[TULIP]s
and
[ROSE]aries

Weeding Out False Doctrine

Travis W. Rogers

Scripture taken (unless otherwise noted) from the NEW AMERICAN STANDARD BIBLE®, Copyright © 1960, 1962, 1963, 1968, 1971, 1972, 1973, 1975, 1977, 1995 by The Lockman Foundation. Used by permission. www.Lockman.org

ISBN-10: 1490325425
ISBN-13: 978-1490325422

DEDICATION

To Pastor Joe Gwynn. Your grasp of the Scriptures is only matched by your love and devotion to the flock. Your love and devotion for the flock is only matched by your longing to see sinners be saved by God's grace. You always have just the right word to say that fits the need of the moment. You are what I desire to be when I grow up. Thank you for the inspiration you have provided in my life as well as your input in the editing of this book.

CONTENTS

ACKNOWLEDGMENTS

I would like to take this moment to thank everybody who took the time to review the manuscript for this book. Your insight was invaluable in the editing process. I would also like to thank my wife, Tiffany, for being so supportive in this process. Naturally, such a project requires time from many people and time is something we all tend to run short on. Without your understanding and patience, I would have never been able to complete this.

INTRODUCTION

While many will undoubtedly see this book as an unnecessary attack on Roman Catholics, I would like to dispel that notion from the beginning. Many of these chapters stemmed from lessons I prepared and delivered years ago. Even then, some walked out in the middle for they were offended at what was being said. It is my sincerest hope that you, the reader, will see past this and find the importance of the topic at hand. We live in a time when everybody has an interpretation and, so long as nobody gets challenged, all is well. Unfortunately, this only leads to masses being led to Hell despite their best intentions. As Dr. John Gerstner once said, "Error is not innocent and every idle thought will be brought into judgment. We must give heed to ourselves how we think. We shall have our interpretations, indeed, but they must be sound interpretations." As you read through this book, it is my prayer that you will use discernment and see for yourselves what God has said to us through the Scriptures. It is my further prayer that you will give heed to the call to stand against false teachers while also standing firm in the ever-precious doctrines of grace.

Travis W. Rogers

Part One
The Root of It All

1 MISSIONARY FIELD OR FAMILY?

What is a Christian? Take a moment to ponder this question. One would think this is a simple question to answer. However, for being so simple, it can be one of the most confusing titles to ever exist. The typical unbeliever thinks we are silly. Atheists think we lack intelligence. Cultists think we are the ones who need to see the light. While it is expected that all these groups would fail to understand things which are spiritually discerned (1 Corinthians 2:14), it never ceases to amaze me how many self-proclaimed Christians are actually confused on the matter. Gather a group of Christians, both new and mature, and ask them what they think it means to be a Christian. You would probably get a wide range of answers but, with almost certainty, they will all hold at least one thing in common. It is almost certain that all or most would claim you must believe Christ was God in the flesh, that he lived a perfect life, died for our sins, and was resurrected on the third day. While this is all very true and is even an essential part of the Gospel, it may surprise you that even certain cults teach most of these points. In fact, James tells us that even the demons believe this much and they shudder (James 2:19)! If one cannot properly articulate what it means to be a Christian, how much more difficult would it be for him to articulate what a Christian looks like? I'm not saying it is impossible but I am saying it becomes exponentially more difficult to understand who is or is not a member of the body of Christ if that person does not have an adequate understanding of the marks of a true believer.

I would like to bring something to the table that has confused many people over the years. It is a topic that has differing views. It is a topic that many people feel they know the basics of but fall short when asked for an explanation. The subject is whether Roman Catholicism should be considered a valid option. The subject is whether Roman Catholics are brothers and sisters in Christ or if they are the mission field. Certainly, one does not have to agree in all areas in order to be a brother or sister in Christ. If this were the case, we would be left wondering who would get to Heaven in the end; Baptists or Methodists, Lutherans or Presbyterians? Is the Roman Catholic Church simply off in secondary issues yet still in the body or are they separated by a great chasm of erroneous doctrine? I want to let it be known that nothing said in this chapter is meant to belittle anybody else as a person. In fact, with the knowledge of what is in the chapter, I would hope it would encourage you to love enough to plant seeds of the Gospel wherever you go. No, this chapter is not meant to spread hate or strife. It is simply meant to inform so that you will never again be without an appropriate response when presented with the question for which this chapter is named after.

Beginning in 1985, there was a movement. This movement was called Evangelicals and Catholics Together (ECT). In 1994, there were many people of both Protestant and Catholic belief who signed an official document. The purpose of the ECT was to work together for the common good. Although they may have their differences, they believed they were following the same Christ. Instead of fighting each other, they desired to work for the common good and share Christ to others. On the surface, this seems like a great idea. If we all worship the same Christ, why not work together? It was a joint effort to stop treating each other like the mission field. However, this simply is not possible regardless what piece of paper is signed so long as each party holds their beliefs unwavering. As sad as it may be to admit, there are simply too many irreconcilable differences.

To realize why it is impossible, a Protestant must only look at his/her own name. The key word is protest. The protest that gave birth to Protestantism was the protest of the Roman Catholic Church. There are some very clear things being protested among Protestants. In fact, the Catholic Church had some very strong things to protest as well toward us. In the 1500's, over the course of 18 years, a council took place to put together an official statement. This assembly was known as the Council of Trent and it convened at the height of the Protestant movement. Protestantism was gaining popularity in the way it held dear to Scripture alone (Sola Scriptura) and did not place Church tradition on the same divine level. The Roman Catholic Church, on the other hand, claimed equal authority for both, with tradition trumping special revelation. This is a practice that continues even today.

Catechism of the Catholic Church, para. 82

> ...the Church, to whom the transmission and interpretation of Revelation is entrusted, does not derive her certainty about all revealed truths from the holy Scriptures alone. Both Scripture and Tradition must be accepted and honored with equal sentiments of devotion and reverence.[i]

The Council of Trent had a purpose to put a stop to the Sola Scriptura Reformers. They declared 125 anathemas in this attempt. Dictionary.com defines anathema as, "a person or thing accursed or consigned to damnation or destruction." In other words, the Roman Catholic Church listed 125 different ways a Protestant is eternally cut off and cursed by God. I will now review a few of those ways.

Canon 9, Justification

> If any one saith, that by faith alone the impious is justified; in such wise as to mean, that nothing else is required to cooperate in order

> to the obtaining the grace of Justification, and that it is not in any way necessary, that he be prepared and disposed by the movement of his own will; let him be anathema.[ii]

In other words, if you believe you are justified by faith alone and that there is no work we can possibly do to justify ourselves, you are eternally cursed and cut off from God. However, this is contrary to the teaching of Scripture. We are justified by faith alone. The Council of Trent's response to this recurring theme in Scripture was to claim, "faith is the first stage of human salvation."[iii]

Romans 3:20

> because by the works of the Law no flesh will be justified in His sight; for through the Law comes the knowledge of sin.

Romans 3:28

> For we maintain that a man is justified by faith apart from works of the Law.

Ephesians 2:8

> For by grace you have been saved through faith; and that not of yourselves, it is the gift of God;

Titus 3:5

> He saved us, not on the basis of deeds which we have done in righteousness, but according to His mercy, by the washing of regeneration and renewing by the Holy Spirit,

Keeping the Law does not justify us. If anything, it does the exact opposite. It shows how there is nothing we can do to justify ourselves.

It shows our total depravity and dependence upon God. It gives us knowledge of sin. It shines light on sin so that we can see it for what it really is and how impossible it is to be justified apart from.

Canon 23, Justification

> If any one saith, that a man once justified can sin no more, nor lose grace, and that therefore he that falls and sins was never truly justified; or, on the other hand, that he is able, during his whole life, to avoid all sins, even those that are venial,- except by a special privilege from God, as the Church holds in regard of the Blessed Virgin; let him be anathema.[iv]

Canon 23 declares it is possible, indeed likely, to lose one's salvation. As James McCarthy says, "In the same day a Catholic can wake up justified, lose the grace of justification through mortal sin, and be justified again through the sacrament of penance."[v] According to the Council of Trent, f you say it is impossible to lose your salvation and that one who falls away from the faith was never truly saved to begin with, be eternally cursed by God. Again, this is in direct violation of what the Scriptures tell us.

1 John 2:19

> They went out from us, but they were not really of us; for if they had been of us, they would have remained with us; but they went out, so that it would be shown that they all are not of us.

John 3:36

> He who believes in the Son has eternal life; but he who does not obey the Son will not see life, but the wrath of God abides on him.

John 6:40

> For this is the will of My Father, that everyone who beholds the Son and believes in Him will have eternal life, and I Myself will raise him up on the last day.

John 10:28

> and I give eternal life to them, and they will never perish; and no one will snatch them out of My hand.

Salvation is not something which is here today and gone tomorrow. It is eternal. What good is eternity if it is only temporary and always changing? The answer is that it isn't. Thankfully, Scripture promises something quite different. It tells us that a man who has obtained salvation through faith will remain secure in his salvation (more in chapter 8). If he departs from his faith, it was to show that he never had faith to begin with for nobody can snatch us out of the Father's hand and Christ will not lose even one of his sheep.

Canon 24, Justification

> If any one saith, that the justice received is not preserved and also increased before God through good works; but that the said works are merely the fruits and signs of Justification obtained, but not a cause of the increase thereof; let him be anathema.[vi]

The Council of Trent declares that good works are not merely the fruit of a Christian but are actually a method of obtaining justification. If you believe the former and not the latter, you are eternally cursed by God. If you believe, as the Scripture teaches, that works are a proof of the salvation which you have already obtained, according to the Roman Catholic Church, you are eternally cursed.

Galatians 3:1-3

You foolish Galatians, who has bewitched you, before whose eyes Jesus Christ was publicly portrayed as crucified? This is the only thing I want to find out from you: did you receive the Spirit by the works of the Law, or by hearing with faith? Are you so foolish? Having begun by the Spirit, are you now being perfected by the flesh?

Galatians 5:1

It was for freedom that Christ set us free; therefore keep standing firm and do not be subject again to a yoke of slavery.

Romans 8:30

and these whom He predestined, He also called; and these whom He called, He also justified; and these whom He justified, He also glorified.

If good works are more than just fruit and do indeed justify, why is it that Paul so clearly states otherwise? Paul tells us we are to not be subject to a yoke of slavery. By putting our faith and hope of justification in works, we are binding ourselves to them. We are hoping we will perform well enough so that we might one day be considered justified. Paul rebukes the Galatians for this. He calls them foolish to think something that was started by the Spirit could be made perfect by our own doing in the flesh. Justification is by Christ alone. Those whom He calls, He justifies. Our own works have nothing to do with it.

Canon 30, Justification

If any one saith, that, after the grace of Justification has been received, to every penitent sinner the guilt is remitted, and the debt of eternal punishment is blotted out in such wise, that there remains not any debt of temporal punishment to be discharged either in this world, or in the next in Purgatory, before the entrance to the kingdom of heaven can be opened (to him); let him be anathema.[vii]

In other words, if you believe the blood of Christ fully cleanses and does not leave some form of spot or blemish in which we must purify ourselves of in the fires of purgatory, you are anathema. If you believe the blood of Christ to be sufficient, you are anathema. If you believe the blood of Christ has covered you completely and made you white as snow, you are anathema!

Colossians 2:13-14

When you were dead in your transgressions and the uncircumcision of your flesh, He made you alive together with Him, having forgiven us all our transgressions, having canceled out the certificate of debt consisting of decrees against us, which was hostile to us; and He has taken it out of the way, having nailed it to the cross.

Colossians 2:10a

and in Him you have been made complete,

Colossians 1:13

For He rescued us from the domain of darkness, and transferred us to the kingdom of His beloved Son,

1 John 2:1

My little children, I am writing these things to you so that you may not sin And if anyone sins, we have an Advocate with the Father, Jesus Christ the righteous; and He Himself is the propitiation for our sins;

We are forgiven of **all** of our transgressions. Christ canceled out all of our debt. He rescued us from the domain of darkness; from Hell. While we are not to sin, even if we do, we have an Advocate in Christ. That is in the current tense. We currently have an Advocate making intercession for us at all times.

John MacArthur

> Here Advocate translates *paraklētos* ("one who comes alongside") and denotes in legal settings the defender or counselor who comes to aid his client...Christ is the perfect Advocate, since the Judge is His Father and they are always in perfect harmony (cf. Matt. 26:39; John 4:34). [viii]

Every little thing that might be held against us is nailed to the cross. As a result, we are fully justified and are left spotless before the eyes of God. Brothers and sisters, do not be confused on this matter!

Canon 3, The Sacrifice of the Mass

> If any one saith, that the sacrifice of the mass is only a sacrifice of praise and of thanksgiving; or, that it is a bare commemoration of the sacrifice consummated on the cross, but not a propitiatory sacrifice; or, that it profits him only who receives; and that it ought not to be offered for the living and the dead for sins, pains, satisfactions, and other necessities; let him be anathema. [ix]

To understand, the Catholic Mass would be similar to our communion. Another name for it is the Eucharist. In other words, if you do not believe that communion is a sacrifice of Jesus, you are condemned. If you do not believe that communion is profitable for the dead as well as the living, you are damned. If you do not believe that communion is a means of propitiation, you are cursed. If you believe communion to be merely symbolic and not the imparting of grace, you are eternally cut off from the Father. Here are some quotes from official Catholic teaching:

New St. Joseph Baltimore Catechism, Vol. 2 Question 357

> The mass is the sacrifice of the new law in which Christ, through the Ministry of the priest, offers himself to God in an unbloody manner under the appearances of bread and wine. The mass is the sacrifice of Christ offered in a sacramental manner...the reality is the same but the appearances differ.

Their catechism clearly teaches that the mass is a sacrifice of Christ. Now the question remains as to what they mean by sacrifice. Thankfully, they answer this question:

New St. Joseph Baltimore Catechism, Vol. 2 Question 358

> A sacrifice is the offering of a victim by a priest to God alone, and the destruction of it in some way to knowledge that he is the creator of all things.

Based on those two statements alone, we can clearly see the mass is the sacrifice of Christ, their victim, which a priest offers up to God countless times over and over again to purposefully destroy him on the altar. Unfortunately, there is more.

Catechism of the Catholic Church, 1369

> The sacrifice of Christ the only Mediator, which in the Eucharist is offered through the priests' hands,[x]

How is it that they can possibly be proud to claim something so vile and disgusting? The Roman Catholic Church attempts to use Scripture to back itself up but it fails miserably. They use verses such as Matthew 26 and Luke 22.

Matthew 26:26-28

> While they were eating, Jesus took some bread, and after a blessing, He broke it and gave it to the disciples, and said, "Take, eat; this is My body." And when He had taken a cup and given thanks, He gave it to them, saying, "Drink from it, all of you; for this is My blood of the covenant, which is poured out for many for forgiveness of sins.

Luke 22:19

> And when He had taken some bread and given thanks, He broke it and gave it to them, saying, "This is My body which is given for you; do this in remembrance of Me."

Instead of taking this as a command to perform communion in remembrance of the death of Christ, the Roman Catholic Church teaches that Christ was passing on a sacrament to the apostles and their succeeding priests and was giving them the power to transform the bread and wine into the literal flesh and blood of Christ. As we read, they do not teach that it is bread and wine but rather, literal flesh and blood that only appears to be bread and wine although the bread and wine is no more.

This is where the priest comes into play with his sacrifice. He goes to the altar where the bread and wine await him. He lifts it up to the sky in the action of raising it to God. He then brings it down and offers it to the people. According to their teaching, it is not bread and wine that he offers up but is literally Christ being sacrificed by the priest under the appearance of bread and wine.

The Catholic Church does not deny that Christ alone is our propitiation. However, with their teaching of the Mass, it allows them to claim propitiation in the act of the priest for it is Christ being sacrificed.

Hebrews 7:26-27

For it was fitting for us to have such a high priest, holy, innocent, undefiled, separated from sinners and exalted above the heavens; who does not need daily, like those high priests, to offer up sacrifices, first for His own sins and then for the sins of the people, because this He did once for all when He offered up Himself.

Hebrews 10:1

For the Law, since it has only a shadow of the good things to come and not the very form of things, can never, by the same sacrifices which they offer continually year by year, make perfect those who draw near.

Hebrews 10:10-12

By this will we have been sanctified through the offering of the body of Jesus Christ once for all. Every priest stands daily ministering and offering time after time the same sacrifices, which can never take away sins; but He, having offered one sacrifice for sins for all time, SAT DOWN AT THE RIGHT HAND OF GOD,

According to Scripture, Christ died once for all. There was no need for countless reoccurrence as was the habit of the priests. We are told the repetitious sacrifices are in vain as they can never take away sins. We are also told that Christ died once for all so who is it that the Catholic priests are sacrificing? It is bad enough that they claim to sacrifice Christ countless times over but it is even worse that they are lifting up someone other than Christ since we know Christ was only sacrificed once and that was by God. Once was sufficient. Once for all. Who are they lifting up in their worship because it is not our Lord?!?!?! The whole concept of the Mass is an extremely anti-biblical, pagan, and dare I say, Satanic practice.

The Catholic Church will deny their claim that they re-sacrifice Christ over and over. They do this because the claim of repetitious sacrificing completely goes against the Scripture that says he was sacrificed once for all. They instead say that they are simply re-presenting the sacrifice of Christ. Despite these claims, this is not what they teach.

Catechism of the Catholic Church, 1068

> For it is in the liturgy, especially in the divine sacrifice of the Eucharist, that "the work of our redemption is accomplished"[xi]

Catechism of the Catholic Church, 1367

> The sacrifice of Christ and the sacrifice of the Eucharist are one single sacrifice[xii]

By their own admission, they go against Scripture. However, they will never claim error because they believe they are preserved from such. They can never be wrong in their doctrine or dogmas. They clearly teach a sacrifice of Christ and will never recant these teachings for to do so would crumble the whole system. If one thing is admitted to be wrong, how many countless other things are wrong as well? Again, if Christ is not being sacrificed over and over again (as per the Scriptures), who is it that they are lifting up week after week all over the world? Now, a Roman Catholic will never admit to such a belief. In fact, I am thoroughly convinced the vast majority of the Roman Catholic Church would be appalled by such an implication. Unfortunately, there are certain outcomes which cannot be avoided should we choose to remain consistent.

Canon 33, Justification

> If any one saith, that, by the Catholic doctrine touching Justification, by this holy Synod inset forth in this present decree, the glory of

> God, or the merits of our Lord Jesus Christ are in any way derogated from, and not rather that the truth of our faith, and the glory in fine of God and of Jesus Christ are rendered (more) illustrious; let him be anathema.[xiii]

In other words, if you disagree with even one jot or tittle of the declarations and teachings of the Catholic priesthood, you are eternally cut off from the glory of Heaven, eternally cursed by God, and are destined for Hell. I must be in big trouble then because I denounce every single one of those and I have the Truth of Scripture to bring me confidence in these matters.

One may ask if the Catholic Church still holds to these teachings. Wouldn't it be highly possible that they would have renounced these absurd teachings so many years after the Reformation? It is clear the whole purpose of them was to scare people from leaving the Roman Catholic Church during a time when so many were converting to Protestantism. Despite this, the Roman Catholic Church still clings to each and every one of the teachings of the Council of Trent. In fact, it was only about 50 years ago that Pope John XXIII affirmed them. To oppose them is to go against the very core of Catholic teaching.

1 Timothy 3:15

> but in case I am delayed, I write so that you will know how one ought to conduct himself in the household of God, which is the church of the living God, the pillar and support of the truth.

Matthew 16:18

> I also say to you that you are Peter, and upon this rock I will build My church; and the gates of Hades will not overpower it.

The Roman Catholic Church teaches that it is Christ's one true church and that they are preserved from error. They claim the truth abides with them and that they will never teach doctrinal error because the gates of Hell will not overpower Christ's Church. Because of this, nothing they declare as doctrine, dogma, anathema, or especially ex cathedra will ever be wrong. While admitting individuals may hold to an erroneous belief, any official declaration from the Church is free from error. As a result, instead of preserving the truth, they have done nothing more than preserve error upon error under a system of works.

We have only unearthed a few of the decrees from the Council of Trent. According to the Roman Catholic teachings, a few other things that will get you booted to Hell include:

1) Rejecting the Apocrypha as being the inspired Word of God

2) Saying baptism is not a requirement for salvation

3) Claim infant baptism is wrong

4) Believe confirmation is just a ceremony and not a sacrament that imputes grace

5) Deny penance

6) Deny the priesthood

7) Deny the doctrine of purgatory

Where exactly does the grace of God ever come into play in all of these preposterous claims?

Cardinal Ratzinger

The Mass is the sum and substance of our faith.[xiv]

If the Mass is the substance of faith, the Catholic Church does not have saving faith. The Mass lifts up someone they call Christ but is not actually Jesus. It worships a counterfeit and makes sacrifice after sacrifice of this counterfeit Christ. Again, how can this be the substance of faith? It follows after a system of legalistic works that teach you can earn your salvation as if by merit so long as you follow their rituals and make payment on time. It teaches that there is some other way of justification and some other source of propitiation and then places it at the feet of the priest who lifts it up to a false god. No, the Catholic Church cannot be considered a valid alternative. It cannot even be defined as a Christian denomination any more than Mormonism or Jehovah's Witnesses can be. Their counterfeit Jesus is not an all sufficient Savior but merely a person who helps them to save themselves.

Dr. Mark Jones

> In the end, our controversy with Rome is important because Christ is important. Christ alone – not He and Mary (LG 62) – intercedes between us and the Father; Christ alone – not the pope (LG 22) – is the head of the church and, thus, the supreme judge of our consciences; Christ alone – not pagan "dictates of conscience" (LG 16) – must be the object of faith for salvation; and Christ's righteousness alone – not ours (LG 40) – is the only hope we have for standing before a God who is both just and Justifier of the wicked. To move to Rome is not only to give up justification and, thus, assurance – even more so, it is to give up Christ.[xv]

Just keep in mind that not all Roman Catholics fully affirm its teachings. Some people know the truth for what it is but do not see the harm in staying in the Catholic church (lowercase "c") they grew up in. Being in a local Catholic Church is not the same as being a follower of the Catholic teaching any more than sitting in a pew on Easter Sunday makes you a Christian. If you know anybody in this predicament, I urge you to speak with them of the importance of leaving. While it may seem harmless, I hope the examples brought to you tonight can show how it is far from it. It is very dangerous and we need to understand why. It is the mission field through and through.

[i] Catholic Church, Catechism of the Catholic Church. [Libreria Editrice Vaticana, 1994] pg. 82

[ii] Council of Trent, session 6, "Decree on Justification," canon 9

[iii] Ibid. canon 8

[iv] Ibid. canon 23

[v] James G. McCarthy, The Gospel According to Rome [Harvest House Publishers, 1995] pg. 104

[vi] Council of Trent, session 6, "Decree on Justification," canon 24

[vii] Ibid. canon 30

[viii] John MacArthur, The MacArthur New Testament Commentary on 1-3 John [Moody Publishers, 2007] pg. 46

[ix] Council of Trent, session 22, "Doctrine on the Sacrifice of the Mass," canon 3

[x] Catholic Church, Catechism of the Catholic Church. [Libreria Editrice Vaticana, 1994] 1369

[xi] Ibid. 1068

[xii] Ibid. 1367

[xiii] Council of Trent, session 6, "Decree on Justification," canon 33

[xiv] As quoted by John MacArthur, "Explaining the Heresy of the Catholic Mass" [http://www.gty.org/resources/sermons/90-318/Explaining-the-Heresy-of-the-Catholic-Mass-Part-1]

[xv] Jones, Mark, "Swimming The Tiber?" Tabletalk Dec. 2012: pg 75

2 DOCTRINES OF ERROR

In the previous chapter, we covered some of the many differences between Roman Catholicism and Protestantism. It is my hope that we are all in agreement on the fact that Roman Catholicism simply is not a valid alternative nor can it be considered a denomination of Christianity. We reviewed their own declarations from the Council of Trent as well as the Catechism.

In this chapter, our focus will be the Scriptural response to some of the other doctrines and dogmas of the Catholic Church. As was the case with chapter 1, this is not meant to belittle anyone simply because they hold to differing beliefs. Very rarely will two people agree on everything. The question is not whether there is disagreement as much as it is whether the essentials of the faith are held to. This alone will be the dividing line in all cases. Remember, we were all once categorized among the fornicators, idolaters, adulterers, effeminate, homosexuals, thieves, the covetous, drunkards, revilers, and swindlers. It is only by the grace of God that we have been washed, sanctified, and justified (1 Corinthians 6:10-11). No, the purpose of this first section is simply meant to point out the differences from a Scriptural perspective to further your understanding of Truth. It is as John Calvin said:

John Calvin to Michael Servetus

> I neither hate you nor despise you; nor do I wish to persecute you; but I would be as hard as iron when I behold you insulting sound doctrine with so great audacity.[i]

John Calvin

> A dog barks when his master is attacked. I would be a coward if I saw that God's truth is attacked and yet would remain silent without giving any sound.[ii]

As always, my goal is to teach the Truth of Scripture in the Light of Scripture alone. Sola Scriptura!

As you continue reading, I pray the Spirit continues to move you in your convictions. There are several points we are going to be covering and, the further we delve in, the more you will see how it builds upon the previous chapter. Our first area we are going to touch on is the doctrine of purgatory.

Catechism of the Catholic Church, para. 1030

> All who die in God's grace and friendship, but still imperfectly purified, are indeed assured of their eternal salvation, but after death they undergo purification, so as to achieve the holiness necessary to enter the joy of Heaven.[iii]

Handbook for Today's Catholic

> If you die in the love of God but possess any stains of sin, such stains are cleansed away in a purifying process called Purgatory. These stains of sin are primarily the temporal punishment due to venial or mortal sins already forgiven but for which sufficient penance was not done during your lifetime.[iv]

According to Roman Catholicism, all men die with a stain of sin. The only exceptions to this are infant babies who have been baptized and the saints who were deemed exceptionally holy. All others are blemished with sin even till the point of death. As a result of this, one cannot enter into the joy of Heaven until they have been purified. This purification is as by fire. Catholicism does not rely primarily on Scripture for this doctrine though they do claim it is a solid Biblical doctrine. Truth be told, it is a doctrine that stems from their own teaching which they refer to as Sacred Tradition. To be fair, it is a subject taught in the Catholic Bible as it will be found in the Apocrypha. Specifically, it stems from 2 Maccabees 12:39-46. The Apocrypha, comprised of several Deuterocanonical books, is included in the Catholic bible but it is not found in the Protestant bible for many reasons. Among other things, the books have been proven false and are laced with contradictions. This is certainly the case with this the Maccabees. Furthermore, there is no direct reference to purgatory and even the story itself is internally inconsistent.[v] Though these negative aspects certainly exist, this is not to say all of the Apocryphal books are entirely useless. They can be used as history lessons of what took place at that time but, in the end, they were written by fallible, uninspired men and are not to be included among the inspired Word of God. However, they have attempted to fit it to Scripture by referencing various passages. One passage in particular is from 1 Corinthians.

1 Corinthians 3:15

> If any man's work is burned up, he will suffer loss; but he himself will be saved, yet so as through fire.

In essence, the doctrine of purgatory teaches that one is to live a good and holy life but that they will eventually end in a state of sin with the need to be purified by fire and cleansed from the stain. Before I get into the doctrine of purgatory as a whole, I'd like to touch on a few other areas. Those areas are penance and indulgences.

Catechism of the Catholic Church, para. 1480

Like all the sacraments, Penance is a liturgical action. The elements of the celebration are ordinarily these: a greeting and blessing from the priest, reading the word of God to illuminate the conscience and elicit contrition, and an exhortation to repentance; the confession, which acknowledges sins and makes them known to the priest; the imposition and acceptance of a penance; the priest's absolution; a prayer of thanksgiving and praise and dismissal with the blessing of the priest. [vi]

Catechism of the Catholic Church, para. 1468

The whole power of the sacrament of Penance consists in restoring us to God's grace and joining us with him in an intimate friendship." Reconciliation with God is thus the purpose and effect of this sacrament. [vii]

In other words, penance is a part of the process of reconciliation. We become reconciled to God through a string of actions on our part. The Catechism of the Catholic Church states that we need to do "something more to make amends for the sin." [viii] We earn the grace of God by the works that we complete on this Earth. According to Catholicism, the proper way to be reconciled to God is by being greeted and blessed by a priest, reading Scripture in public, and confessing our sins to a priest. It is by this method that one can attempt to achieve a state of holiness so as to reduce the amount of time they have to spend in purgatory. After all, isn't the goal to get to Heaven as soon as possible?

All of this ties into indulgences. While penance is the active process of sanctification and obtaining holiness and good graces of God, indulgences are the method of obtaining forgiveness for sins already committed. It is not actually a way of obtaining forgiveness of the sin itself but rather a method of spiritual stain removal. Penance is preventative whereas indulgences are corrective. Indulgences come in two forms. Depending on the method through which it is obtained, one can be granted either a partial indulgence or a plenary indulgence. Partial indulgences are the removal of only a part of the temporal punishment due to sin whereas plenary indulgences are for the complete remission of all temporal punishment stored up at that time. The former can come through such manners as praying the Rosary whereas the latter involves praying the Rosary, receiving the sacraments of confession and Eucharist, and offering prayers for the Pope's intentions.[ix] Like penance, indulgences are meant to reduce the amount of time one has to spend in purgatory. This is done by drawing from what is known as the Treasury of the Church. Just as the Roman Catholic faith is based upon works, these same works are stored in a heavenly storehouse where merit can be drawn from by members of the Church. However, all drawings of indulgences are given through the Church by its priests through official sacraments.

Second Vatican Council

> The "treasury of the Church" is the infinite value, which can never be exhausted, which Christ's merits have before God. They were offered so that the whole of mankind could be set free from sin and attain communion with the Father. In Christ, the Redeemer himself, the satisfactions and merits of his Redemption exist and find their efficacy. This treasury includes as well the prayers and good works of the Blessed Virgin Mary. They are truly immense, unfathomable and even pristine in their value before God. In the treasury, too, are the prayers and good works of all the saints, all those who have followed in the footsteps of Christ the Lord and by his grace have made their lives holy and carried out the mission of the Father entrusted to them. In this way they attained their own salvation and at the same time cooperated in saving their brothers in the unity of the Mystical Body.[x]

Now that we have an idea of what penance, indulgences, and purgatory are, let's look at Scripture to see what the Word of God says.

Penance and indulgences are both a form of works based salvation. It denies the atonement of Christ and places it in the hands of the priests. Regarding penance, the Catholic Church tells us we can perform works to earn justification and be considered righteous.

Romans 4:3

For what does the Scripture say? "ABRAHAM BELIEVED GOD, AND IT WAS CREDITED TO HIM AS RIGHTEOUSNESS."

Romans 5:9

Much more then, having now been justified by His blood, we shall be saved from the wrath of God through Him.

Romans 5:1

Therefore, having been justified by faith, we have peace with God through our Lord Jesus Christ,

Romans 4:5

Now to the one who works, his wage is not credited as a favor, but as what is due. But to the one who does not work, but believes in Him who justifies the ungodly, his faith is credited as righteousness,

Galatians 2:16

nevertheless knowing that a man is not justified by the works of the Law but through faith in Christ Jesus, even we have believed in Christ Jesus, so that we may be justified by faith in Christ and not by the works of the Law; since by the works of the Law no flesh will be justified.

Scripture is very clear when it says we are not saved by our works nor is there anything we can do to justify ourselves. It is by faith alone through the blood of Christ. We are not justified by penance and indulgences. We are justified by his blood. The doctrine of penance and indulgences clearly detracts from the atonement provided in the blood of Christ. It removes the sufficiency of Christ and amounts it to nothing more than a fraction of plan of salvation.

I'll have you know, John battled a group of people similar to this.

1 John 5:13

These things I have written to you who believe in the name of the Son of God, so that you may know that you have eternal life.

John was combating a particular error in his day. They were the Gnostics. They taught of a secret knowledge that was pertinent to salvation that only they could reveal. John speaks boldly and bluntly in his use of the word "know." He wanted the readers to understand that there was no hidden knowledge regarding salvation. It was cut and dry. They could KNOW whether or not they were saved. They could be confident! The Roman Catholic Church functions in much the same way. They say outside of the Catholic Church, there is no preservation from error. They say outside the Catholic Church, one cannot be saved. Sure, this is not the spoken word taught today but it is to be understood so long as they affirm the declarations of the Council of Trent that we went over in chapter 1. They teach that they have a hidden knowledge that is preserved within their church; that they claim to be Christ's only Church. It is only through the priests that this knowledge and revelation can be shared and experienced. It is modern Gnosticism in more ways than one.

Not only are indulgences unbiblical, they were also created as a money making scandal. In the early Church, indulgences were often sold to the people. The people would bring the priests money and the priests would then offer up indulgences on their behalf. These indulgences would often be purchased for the dead in a hope to speed up their time in purgatory so they could enjoy the joy of Heaven. Indulgences were sold in the form of time periods. There were basic indulgences sold during the Mass that would shave time off of purgatory for basic sins. Then there were more expensive indulgences offered by bishops. These would only be available to certain people in higher financial standing. Of course, if it meant getting to Heaven faster, losing money was a trivial concern. Because a man's heart is only known by God, it was unknown how long one would spend in purgatory. Therefore, Catholics would go over and over just in case. Again, it only made sense to keep paying for indulgences in hopes that you would free your dead loved ones from the fires of purgatory as well as avoid having to go there yourself. As long as you pay, you can enjoy the joys of Heaven in an expedient manner. So long as you perform works in the Church, purgatory will go by much faster than for others. However, if you really care about the others, you can help them out by paying some more. This is the grim reality of how it all started. Things may have changed over the years but the roots still remain.

All of this leads to the concept of purgatory and how it completely bashes the concept of grace and forgiveness in Christ. Since we already covered the basics of what purgatory is all about, I now want to go over the Scriptural response.

Romans 8:1

Therefore there is now no condemnation for those who are in Christ Jesus.

2 Corinthians 5:8

we are of good courage, I say, and prefer rather to be absent from the body and to be at home with the Lord.

As Christians, when our time comes to be absent from the body, there is no fear that we will go anywhere other than at home to be with our precious Lord and Savior. Paul had no fear of death. He knew the moment he left his body, he would be at home with the Lord experiencing the joy of Heaven.

John 19:30

> Therefore when Jesus had received the sour wine, He said, "It is finished!" And He bowed His head and gave up His spirit.

The Greek word used here is *teleo*. Regarding monetary matters, the word was used to refer to a payment of debt. Christ was saying that all debt was considered paid in full. Through his blood, there is no more debt. Why is it that the Catholic Church teaches otherwise?

Hebrews 9:27

> And inasmuch as it is appointed for men to die once and after this comes judgment,

This verse looks like it could almost be used to justify purgatory. Isn't it saying there is judgment after death? Can't it support the notion of God judging us to an intermediate place of purgatory to be cleansed of the stain of our sins? Most certainly not! That is what the blood of Christ perfected.

Upon death, there will indeed be judgment from God. For the unsaved, this judgment will end in eternal death and suffering of Hell. For the saved, this judgment will result in eternal life with the Father. However, our works will be judged as well. They may not play a part in our timeline from death to Heaven but they most certainly affect our rewards in Heaven (2 Corinthians 5:10).

I say all this to bring us back to 1 Corinthians 3:15. As this is a key verse in the Roman Catholic doctrine of purgatory, it deserves special attention. What is the fire Paul speaks of?

1 Corinthians 3:15

> If any man's work is burned up, he will suffer loss; but he himself will be saved, yet so as through fire.

Instead of attempting to find out the meaning of 1 Corinthians 3:15, the Roman Catholic Church invents a meaning in order to make it fit their pre-existing doctrine of purgatory. It is dangerous practice to invent doctrine and then make Scripture fit. If it is not explicitly in Scripture, it is to be excluded.

Again, Paul is not saying one must be purified in purgatory. He is relating the common method of purification to eternal rewards. In those days, fire was the method of removing the dross. Dross is all the waste product of metals being purified in fire. Let's look at the entire passage.

1 Corinthians 3:10-15

> According to the grace of God which was given to me, like a wise master builder I laid a foundation, and another is building on it. But each man must be careful how he builds on it. For no man can lay a foundation other than the one which is laid, which is Jesus Christ. Now if any man builds on the foundation with gold, silver, precious stones, wood, hay, straw, each man's work will become evident; for the day will show it because it is to be revealed with fire, and the fire itself will test the quality of each man's work. If any man's work which he has built on it remains, he will receive a reward. If any man's work is burned up, he will suffer loss; but he himself will be saved, yet so as through fire.

Notice it is not saying that a man must perform works or else be saved through the fires of purgatory. If you notice further, it is evident he isn't even speaking of Christians in general. In verse 10, Paul references the foundation he has laid. While another had begun building upon his foundation, he clearly points out that "no man can lay a foundation other than the one which is laid, which is Jesus Christ." So, again, who is saved as through fire and what does it mean? Paul is referencing the church builders. He is speaking of the importance of laying a strong foundation on Christ. He is urging the church builders to ensure they build the foundation with imperishable items (Numbers 31:22-23) while warning that there will be many who attempt to build churches with wood, hay, and straw. It is these latter men who will one day realize they have nothing to show for all their hard work. While this is not a call for Christians to work hard (though this is a theme we repeatedly see elsewhere in Scripture), it certainly is not justification for purgatory. It is saying that, on the last day, each builder's work will be tested.

One day the judgment of God will come to all. The atoning blood of Christ is the only thing that can save. This will be the first step. Among Christians, however, there is yet another judgment. This judgment will determine the eternal rewards in Heaven.

Matthew 6:20

> But store up for yourselves treasures in heaven, where neither moth nor rust destroys, and where thieves do not break in or steal;

1 Peter 1:7

> so that the proof of your faith, being more precious than gold which is perishable, even though tested by fire, may be found to result in praise and glory and honor at the revelation of Jesus Christ;

Isaiah 64:6a

> For all of us have become like one who is unclean,

> And all our righteous deeds are like a filthy garment;

Outside of Christ, even our greatest works are as filthy rags. In the Hebrew, this literally meant the rags used to catch the bloody flow of a menstruating woman. However, when we have Christ as our foundation, those works take on a whole new meaning. They may not purify us, speed up entrance to Heaven, or work off past sins of others but they do indeed build up treasures in Heaven.

2 Peter 3:10

> But the day of the Lord will come like a thief, in which the heavens will pass away with a roar and the elements will be destroyed with intense heat, and the earth and its works will be burned up.

In the day of judgment, the works of the world will be burned up. The only works to remain will be the eternal works which have been done in Christ. 1 Corinthians chapter 3 used the analogy of gold, silver, and precious stones to relate to a strong foundation built on Christ. It is only this quality which will remain. The works of the world are as wood, hay, and straw. The latter will burn away but works in Christ will remain forever. How then can money be used to buy pardons? As we already covered, we have complete justification and forgiveness of debt in the atoning blood of Christ. Even if a man has saving faith but has only a few works in Christ to go along with it, he will be spared from the fires of judgment simply by being clothed in Christ. His eternal reward will be small but salvation in Christ was still accomplished.

Romans 5:1

> Therefore, having been justified by faith, we have peace with God through our Lord Jesus Christ,

Romans 3:28

> For we maintain that a man is justified by faith apart from works of the Law.

We are justified by faith alone. The Roman Catholic Church teaches we must work for justification, work for Heaven, and experience suffering by fire in order to reach Heaven.

John Murray

> According to Romish theology, all past sins both as respects their eternal and temporal punishments are blotted out in baptism and also the eternal punishment of the future sins of the faithful. But for the temporal punishment of the post-baptismal sins the faithful must make satisfaction either in this life or in purgatory. In opposition to every such notion of human satisfaction Protestants rightly contend that the satisfaction of Christ is the only satisfaction for sin and is so perfect and final that it leaves no penal liability for any sin of the believer. [xi]

Christ said it himself. It is finished! Roman Catholic teaching does not believe this and, in turn, adds to the gospel.

Galatians 1:8-9

> But even if we, or an angel from heaven, should preach to you a gospel contrary to what we have preached to you, he is to be accursed! As we have said before, so I say again now, if any man is preaching to you a gospel contrary to what you received, he is to be accursed!

Anything added to the Gospel is a false gospel. Anything that adds to the finished work of Christ is a false gospel. A false gospel is to be condemned. As I said in the beginning:

John Calvin

A dog barks when his master is attacked. I would be a coward if I saw that God's truth is attacked and yet would remain silent without giving any sound.[xii]

And again, as John Murray so accurately puts it:

John Murray

This polemic against Romish blasphemy is just as necessary today as it was in the Reformation period. The atonement is a completed work, never repeated and unrepeatable.[xiii]

---

[i] Paul Henry, The Life and Times of John Calvin: The Great Reformer, Volume 2 [Nabu Press, 2011] pg. 180

[ii] Martin H. Manser, The Westminster Collection of Christian Quotations [Westminster John Knox Press; 1st edition, 2001] pg. 56

[iii] Catholic Church, Catechism of the Catholic Church. [Libreria Editrice Vaticana, 1994] 1030

[iv] Handbook for Today's Catholic [Liguori Publications, 1984] pg. 47

[v] James G. McCarthy, The Gospel According to Rome [Harvest House Publishers, 1995] pg. 109

[vi] Catholic Church, Catechism of the Catholic Church. [Libreria Editrice Vaticana, 1994] 1480

[vii] Ibid. 1468

[viii] Ibid. 1459

[ix] James G. McCarthy, The Gospel According to Rome [Harvest House Publishers, 1995] pg. 206

[x] Second Vatican Council, "Sacred Liturgy," "Apostolic Constitution on the Revision of Indulgences," No. 5

[xi] John Murray, Redemption: Accomplished and Applied [Wm. B. Eerdmans Publishing Company, 1955] pg. 51

[xii] Martin H. Manser, The Westminster Collection of Christian Quotations [Westminster John Knox Press; 1st edition, 2001] pg. 56

[xiii] John Murray, Redemption: Accomplished and Applied [Wm. B. Eerdmans Publishing Company, 1955] pg. 53

Part Two
The Beauty of TULIP

Travis W. Rogers

3 HISTORY OF CALVINISM

Before one can properly understand a topic, it is a good idea to first gain an understanding of its background and how it came to be. We have already reviewed the many false teachings of the Roman Catholic Church. While many replaced truth with their error, there were still many others who saw through it and recognized it was time for reform. To ignore the call would be a great injustice to God yet to accept would mean a challenge few of us will ever face in our lifetime.

In the previous two chapters, we covered the errors and fallacies of the Roman Catholic Church. For centuries, the Church had slipped away into an impersonal system of religion that focused on power and authority. Simply put, Christ was no longer alive but was left hanging in the crucifix. His sacrifice was not complete as is indicated by the reoccurrence of the Mass. Justification was no longer by grace alone, in Christ alone, through faith alone. The very basics of the simplicity of the Gospel had been perverted to a point to where they were almost unrecognizable.

It was time for reform. Though there had been many in history past who stood up for truth against all odds, God had, in His sovereign timing, selected the sixteenth century as the time He would lift up a great many soldiers to reform the visible Church. Truth be told, it was not Martin Luther's desire to cause division or split the Church down the middle. Had he had his way, the Roman Catholic Church simply would have been expunged of all error and carried on in the Truth. Unfortunately for him, this was not in God's plan.

At the heart of the Reformation was justification by faith alone. This was a major change in doctrine compared to what the Roman Catholic Church had taught for centuries. It was a topic of utmost importance as it dealt with the origin of salvation and the roles of God & man. In a very broad sense, there are two basic categories that are used to ascribe the salvation of man: Monergism and Synergism.

Monergism is a system which claims all of salvation, from beginning to end, is a gracious act of God. It requires no human will for, indeed, the human will would only reject the things of God for it cannot possibly understand that which is Spiritually discerned (1 Corinthians 2:14). On the flip side, we have a system known as Synergism. Synergism claims that both God and man have active roles in salvation and that, without a joint effort, neither God nor man will be reconciled. The Holy Spirit may call a man to Himself but, unless that man accepts the call, he will be lost in his sins. Thus, salvation is combined effort.

One can carry on forever regarding the differences between Roman Catholicism and Protestantism. Indeed, we have over 700 years of history to discuss if we truly want to go into great detail. As it stands, the pages of this book cannot hold it all. I believe, by now, we can adequately understand why the Reformation was necessary and how it has impacted the Church. The end result was the return of a Christ-centered Gospel, Christ-centered justification, and Christ-centered living. I pray we, with the Reformers, can gladly affirm salvation is revealed through Scripture alone (sola Scriptura) and is obtained by grace alone (sola gratia) through faith alone (sola fide) in Christ alone (solus Christus) and all glory goes to God alone (soli Deo Gloria).

Over the next five chapters, we will be covering what has come to be known as the Five Points of Calvinism. Calvinism is a broad subject but is often summarized by five individual points (that are truly one cumulative point). Over the following chapters, we will be covering each of the five points in depth. Before we begin dissecting Calvinism, we need to learn the basics.

1) John Calvin (1509 – 1564)
2) Jacobus Arminius (1560 – 1609)

In 1610, the followers of Arminius, known as the Remonstrants, drafted five points that were based on his teachings in a document aptly titled the Remonstrance of 1610. They requested that the Church of Holland change their doctrines to match the teachings summarized in the five points of what we now know as Arminianism. In turn, the Synod of Dort took place over a period of seven months from 1618-1619 to discuss the Remonstrance. They constructed a document known as the Canons of Dort. It contained four sections that addressed each of the five points brought forth by the Remonstrants. The "canons contain fifty-nine articles of exposition and thirty-four rejections of error."[i] Though not originally in the below order, the sections have been adapted into the acrostic TULIP and has become the most popular summarization of Calvinism to date. By the end of this book, you should have a better grasp of each of the below points:

Total Depravity

Unconditional Election

Limited Atonement

Irresistible Grace

Perseverance of the Saints

J.I. Packer really says it all when comparing the two doctrines:

J.I. Packer

The difference between them is not primarily one of emphasis, but of content. One proclaims a God Who saves; the other speaks of a God Who enables man to save himself. One view presents the three great acts of the Holy Trinity for the recovering of lost mankind – election by the Father, redemption by the Son, calling by the Spirit – as directed towards the same persons, and as securing their salvation infallibly. The other view gives each act a different reference (the objects of redemption being all mankind, of calling, those who hear the gospel, and of election, those hearers who respond), and denies that any man's salvation is secured by any of them. The two theologies thus conceive the plan on salvation in quite different terms. One makes salvation depend on the work of God, the other on a work of man; one regards faith as a part of God's gift of salvation, the other as man's own contribution to salvation; one gives all glory of saving believers to God, the other divides the praise between God, Who, so to speak, built the machinery of salvation, and man, who by believing operated it. Plainly, these differences are important, and the permanent value of the "five points," as a summary of Calvinism, is that they make clear the points at which, and the extent to which, these two conceptions are at variance.[ii]

He continues to go on about how Calvinism is not truly five points but rather, one point. The one true point was only broken into five points to address each of the five points of Arminianism at the Synod of Dort.

J.I. Packer

The very act of setting out Calvinistic soteriology [the doctrine of salvation] in the form of five distinct points tends to obscure the organic character of Calvinistic thought on this subject. For the five points, though separately stated, are really inseparable. They hang together; you cannot reject one without rejecting them all, at least in the sense in which the Synod meant them. For to Calvinism there is really only one point to be made in the field of soteriology: the point that God saves sinners. God – the Triune Jehovah, Father,

Son, and Spirit; three Persons working together in sovereign wisdom, power, and love to achieve the salvation of a chosen people, the Father electing, the Son fulfilling the Father's will by redeeming, the Spirit executing the purpose of Father and Son by renewing. Saves – does everything, first to last, that is involved in bringing man from death in sin to life in glory: plans, achieves and communicates redemption, calls and keeps, justifies, sanctifies, glorifies. Sinners – men as God finds them, guilty, vile, helpless, powerless, unable to lift a finger to do God's will or better their spiritual lot. God saves sinners – and the force of this confession may not be weakened by disrupting the unity of the work of the Trinity, or by dividing the achievement of salvation between God and man and making the decisive part man's own, or by soft-pedaling the sinner's inability so as to allow him to share the praise of his salvation with his Savior. This is the one point of Calvinistic soteriology which the "five points" are concerned to establish and Arminianism in all its forms to deny: namely, that sinners do not save themselves in any sense at all, but that salvation, first and last, whole and entire, past, present, and future, is of the Lord, to whom be glory for ever, Amen.[iii]

As we prepare to venture through each of the five points of Calvinism, you may find yourself riding the fence as do many evangelical Christians today. There are some who choose to set these doctrines aside or minimize their importance in an effort to stay unified with their brothers and sisters in Christ. While this is a noble intention, it is highly impractical if we are to grow in our faith. Can we set aside our understanding of God's sovereignty and still glorify Him? Can we authorize the Spirit to perform and action which the Father Himself has not authorized? Where does avoiding contention slip into the watering down of the Gospel?

Charles Spurgeon

There is no such thing as preaching Christ and Him crucified unless we preach what is nowadays called Calvinism. It is a nickname to call it Calvinism; Calvinism is the Gospel and nothing else. I do not believe that we preach the Gospel unless we preach the sovereignty of God in His dispensation of grace; nor unless we exalt the electing, unchangeable, eternal, immutable, conquering love of Jehovah, not do I think we can preach the Gospel unless we base it upon the special and particular redemption of His elect and chosen people which Christ wrought out upon the cross; nor can I comprehend the Gospel which allows saints to fall away after they are called.[iv]

[i] Joel R. Beeke, Living for God's Glory: An Introduction to Calvinism [Reformation Trust Publishing, 2008] pg. 26

[ii] J.I. Packer, Introductory Essay, pp. 4-5

[iii] Ibid. pg. 6

[iv] Spurgeon, Spurgeon, and Herald, C.H. Spurgeon's Autobiography, Vol. 1, pg. 172

4 TOTAL DEPRAVITY

Walk down the street of your typical city in America and ask several people whether or not they believe they will be going to Heaven. Of those who affirm this, ask them why they believe this. There is a very strong chance that each one will claim it is because he is a "good person." The sad truth of it all is that God's standard of good and man's standard of good are not in the same category whatsoever. Scripture is very clear that only God is good (Mark 10:18) and that every man falls short of such a standard (Romans 3:23).

While men trust in their own wisdom (1 Corinthians 1:21), Total Depravity teaches the exact opposite. It teaches that a man has no good within himself. It teaches that man is wicked, wretched, dead in sin, corrupt, and perverse. Total depravity can also be called total inability; within one's self, there is absolutely zero ability to be saved. Just as man is completely unable to fly, he is also completely unable to perform any act pertaining to salvation.

Westminster Confession of Faith

Man, by his fall into a state of sin, hath wholly lost all ability of will to any spiritual good accompanying salvation; so as, a natural man, being altogether averse from that good, and dead in sin, is not able,

> by his own strength, to convert himself, or to prepare himself
> thereunto.

Please note that just because man is totally depraved, it does not mean he is utterly depraved. Possibly the greatest reason so many reject this doctrine is not because they are repulsed by it but because they do not properly understand it. Nowhere does it teach that we are incapable of performing good deeds as the world judges goodness. Total Depravity does not resign all men to be murderers, rapists, or the like.

Joel R. Beeke

> The Bible tells us that although fallen man is capable of doing some externally good acts, he cannot do anything truly good or pleasing in God's sight (Rom. 8:8) unless he is regenerated by the Holy Spirit (John 3:1-8). From God's standpoint, which is the only true standpoint, natural man is incapable of goodness in thought, word, or deed, and thus cannot contribute anything to his salvation. He is in total rebellion against God.[i]

While the Reformation brought us away from the corruption of the Roman Catholic Church and brought us back in line with Scripture, there will always be false teaching at every point along the way. As we covered in the last chapter, Arminianism is one of the most prominent teachings in our current day and age, especially in America. Many have bought into the lie because it helps us to retain our own power and free will which is a concept that many are not comfortable parting with. However, what does the concept of free will really accomplish other than rendering God's will impotent? As Charles Spurgeon has said, "It declares God's purposes a nullity, since they cannot be carried out unless men are willing. It makes God's will a waiting servant to the will of man."[ii]

Charles Spurgeon

In the day that Adam did eat that fruit his soul died; his imagination lost its mighty power to climb into celestial things and see heaven, his will lost its power always to choose that which is good, his judgment lost all ability to judge between right and wrong decidedly and infallibly, though something was retained in conscience; his memory became tainted, liable to hold evil things, and let righteous things glide away; every power of him creased as to its moral vitality. Goodness was the vitality of his powers - that departed. Virtue, holiness, integrity, these were the life of man; but when these departed man became dead.[iii]

As we dissect the five points, I am hoping you will all see Scripture for what it really says; that all glory is God's alone.

Romans 5:12

Therefore, just as through one man sin entered into the world, and death through sin, and so death spread to all men, because all sinned--

Ephesians 2:1

And you were dead in your trespasses and sins,

Genesis 8:21b

for the intent of man's heart is evil from his youth;

Jeremiah 17:9

The heart is more deceitful than all else
And is desperately sick;
Who can understand it?

John 3:19

> This is the judgment, that the Light has come into the world, and men loved the darkness rather than the Light, for their deeds were evil.

Simply put, we are dead in our sins prior to the washing and regeneration of the Spirit. We are not merely bruised. Romans 5 paints a vivid picture of both Adam and Christ acting as our representative. In the Fall, sin was not merely contained to the Garden of Eden. It was not wrapped up tight waiting for someone to open the box. When Adam sinned, the very nature of all of mankind died on the spot. We became slaves to sin.

Joel R. Beeke

> Consider this literally for a moment. A slave was his master's property. A slave had no time, property, or wealth of his own. He had no single moment of which he could say, "This moment is mine; my master has no rights over this moment." He was always his master's property; his every movement, his every talent, his every possession was entirely his master's. So, Paul says, you were by nature the slaves of sin (Rom. 6:16). Sin was your master. Sin lorded itself over you. Sin was in control. And yet, sin gave the impression all the while that you were free and in charge of your own destiny.[iv]

Sin is a device of Satan, the most crafty of them all. It has ways of ruling over us while we believe we rule ourselves. It has ways of making us believe we are good when, in fact, we are maintaining a path of unrighteousness. We all have the imputed unrighteousness of Adam but, without the imputed righteousness of Christ, we will all continue to fall short while trusting in our own wisdom. Total Depravity "is not simply the absence of righteousness, but the presence of corruption."[v]

Our natural inclinations are so far set against God that we will never properly understand the extent of our sin without the guidance of the Spirit. Indeed, man cannot understand the things of the Spirit without the Spirit first residing in him. In order for the Spirit to reside in him, he must first be regenerated to the point where his body is the temple of God.

1 Corinthians 2:14

But a natural man does not accept the things of the Spirit of God, for they are foolishness to him; and he cannot understand them, because they are spiritually appraised.

1 Corinthians 6:19

Or do you not know that your body is a temple of the Holy Spirit who is in you, whom you have from God, and that you are not your own?

Titus sums is up quite nicely:

Titus 1:15

To the pure, all things are pure; but to those who are defiled and unbelieving, nothing is pure, but both their mind and their conscience are defiled.

We are at war with God and hate Him. Before God calls us to Him, we serve Satan. We have no desire to serve God nor can we possibly desire it because every fiber of our being is against Him.

John 3:20a

For everyone who does evil hates the Light

John 8:44

> You are of your father the devil, and you want to do the desires of
> your father

Romans 3:9-12

> What then? Are we better than they? Not at all; for we have already
> charged that both Jews and Greeks are all under sin;
> as it is written,
> "THERE IS NONE RIGHTEOUS, NOT EVEN ONE;
> THERE IS NONE WHO UNDERSTANDS,
> THERE IS NONE WHO SEEKS FOR GOD;
> ALL HAVE TURNED ASIDE, TOGETHER THEY HAVE BECOME
> USELESS;
> THERE IS NONE WHO DOES GOOD,
> THERE IS NOT EVEN ONE."

All of the above passages confirm our fallen state. Many will agree with this. The area of contention really stems from the belief of whether or not a man has any power whatsoever to do anything about it. Even Jacob Arminius taught that man was totally depraved. However, he held to the belief that God gave everybody enough grace to reverse his own condition if only he believes of his own uncoerced will. It sounds beautiful on the surface but biblical Christianity is not merely a surface level treatment. It is a God honoring practice through the leadership of the Spirit. Is man really as helpless as Calvinism teaches? Are we really so dead in sin that we cannot even choose Christ of our own doing? How dead does Paul mean in Ephesians?

Job 14:4

> Who can make the clean out of the unclean?
> No one!

Jeremiah 13:23

Can the Ethiopian change his skin
Or the leopard his spots?
Then you also can do good
Who are accustomed to doing evil.

John 6:44

No one can come to Me unless the Father who sent Me draws him;
and I will raise him up on the last day.

Many claim an active role in their salvation. Instead of giving full glory to God, they try to cling to some sliver of control by saying they made the choice to be saved. While it sounds nice and many claim it is what the Bible teaches based on its many passages of choosing, it is not accurate. The Bible would never teach a doctrine that would steal glory from God and place it in the hands of men. To say we chose God is to effectively say we saved ourselves. It is to say God was not in full control of the situation and that all the above verses are a lie.

1 Corinthians 4:7

For who regards you as superior? What do you have that you did not receive? And if you did receive it, why do you boast as if you had not received it?

2 Corinthians 3:5

Not that we are adequate in ourselves to consider anything as coming from ourselves, but our adequacy is from God,

Salvation has nothing to do with anything that came from us. For us to claim that we chose God instead of rejecting God means that we took an active part in our salvation. With such an active part, we would have much to boast about but we are told that we've got nothing. We are told that we received salvation and that we have nothing to boast about because it was not of ourselves in any way. Our entire adequacy of salvation is from God alone. We are totally depraved and incapable to seeking God. To Him be the glory!

[i] Joel R. Beeke, Living for God's Glory: An Introduction to Calvinism [Reformation Trust Publishing, 2008] pp. 51-52

[ii] Charles Spurgeon, The Metropolitan Tabernacle Pulpit, Vol. IX [Pasadena, Texas: Pilgrim Publications, 1970, 1973, 1975, 1979] pp. 187

[iii] Charles Spurgeon, The New Park Street Pulpit, Vol. 1, pg. 397

[iv] Joel R. Beeke, Living for God's Glory: An Introduction to Calvinism [Reformation Trust Publishing, 2008] pp. 55

[v] Ibid. pg. 56

5 UNCONDITIONAL ELECTION

By now, you should have at least a grasp of what one is talking about when they mention the term "Calvinism." In this chapter, we will be covering the second point: Unconditional Election. Election is not really a foreign thought to either side of the argument. Most will admit that God has elected those who will be saved. With a number of passages that speak of God's predestination, admitting its presence is not rare at all. The area of contention is whether God's election was the cause or the effect. In other words, did He predestine you unto salvation from history past, not based on anything within you but, based on His own desires and decrees or was there something He saw in you?

Again, the doctrine of election is not usually argued as it is very clear in Scripture as a whole. It isn't until we start to figure out what election is really all about that people come up with different ideas. As usual, my goal is to let Scripture speak for itself.

Psalm 65:4

> How blessed is the one whom You choose and bring near to You
> To dwell in Your courts
> We will be satisfied with the goodness of Your house,

Your holy temple.

Psalm 106:5

That I may see the prosperity of Your chosen ones,
That I may rejoice in the gladness of Your nation,
That I may glory with Your inheritance.

Some may say these are only Old Testament verses that only relate to Israel. I take this point and match it with God's Word.

Matthew 11:27b

nor does anyone know the Father except the Son, and anyone to whom the Son wills to reveal Him.

Matthew 22:14

For many are called, but few are chosen.

By now, you should all be able to see a pattern of at least some type of choosing occurring on God's part. Now, to move into where we get the word "elect" from.

Matthew 24:22, 24, & 31

Unless those days had been cut short, no life would have been saved; but for the sake of the elect those days will be cut short...For false Christs and false prophets will arise and will show great signs and wonders, so as to mislead, if possible, even the elect...And He will send forth His angels with A GREAT TRUMPET and THEY WILL GATHER TOGETHER His elect from the four winds, from one end of the sky to the other.

Luke 18:7

> now, will not God bring about justice for His elect who cry to Him day and night, and will He delay long over them?

Titus 1:1

> Paul, a bond-servant of God and an apostle of Jesus Christ, for the faith of those chosen of God and the knowledge of the truth which is according to godliness,

Again, this is not normally the issue. The issue comes from people who believe that God chose them based on knowing they would freely choose Him at some point in their life. From what we know of our depraved and corrupt nature, we can confidently say it is impossible for one to freely choose God because Scripture is clear that no one seeks God, no one chooses God, and no one does good. We are totally depraved beings before God takes hold of us. We are set apart from God and dead in our sin. Keep this in mind as we go through the following verses that normally mislead people on the surface.

Romans 8:28-30

> And we know that God causes all things to work together for good to those who love God, to those who are called according to His purpose. For those whom He foreknew, He also predestined to become conformed to the image of His Son, so that He would be the firstborn among many brethren; and these whom He predestined, He also called; and these whom He called, He also justified; and these whom He justified, He also glorified.

1 Peter 1:1-2a

> Peter, an apostle of Jesus Christ, To those...who are chosen according to the foreknowledge of God the Father, by the sanctifying

> work of the Spirit, to obey Jesus Christ and be sprinkled with His
> blood:

With passages like the two above, it is easy to infer that God only chooses us based on His foreknowledge. After all, doesn't Romans 8:29 say God predestined those whom He foreknew? Doesn't 1 Peter 1:2 say that God chooses according to His foreknowledge? Is it really so far of a stretch to claim that God foresaw that we would respond with gladness to the universal call of the Gospel? What if He saw that we would choose Him and then predestined us based on our own choices? Sam Storms, founder of Enjoying God Ministries, has said, "The question reduces to this: Does God elect people because they believe in the Lord Jesus Christ [Arminianism], or does God elect people in order that they shall believe in Christ [Calvinism]?"[i]

Let us begin to answer these with another question. If God based salvation on His advance knowledge of those who would believe, where did their saving faith come from? We know that the natural man does not choose God.

John 8:44

> You are of your father the devil, and you want to do the desires of
> your father

Scripture has a tendency to be blunt in many cases. This is one of them. It leaves no room for argument regarding the natural man. While 1 Corinthians tells us the natural man cannot understand the things of the Spirit of God, John goes a step further by saying we are children of the devil. He is our father and he is our master. We live to serve his desires and we do so gladly because it is our own deepest desire. The desire of the devil is certainly not for us to choose God. Because of the Scripture alone that we covered last chapter, one cannot Scripturally come to the conclusion that man, of his own carnal & unsaved self, chooses Christ. This means the foreknowledge that Romans & 1 Peter speaks of cannot imply knowledge of who would choose God. This interpretation is contradictory at best and serves no other purpose than to confuse us while we cling to every last shred of control and free will. As it stands, this is no proper way to interpret the Word of God. The proper context is speaking of God ordaining in advance before the foundation of the world.

1 Peter 1:20

> For He was foreknown before the foundation of the world,

Here we see Christ being referred to as foreknown. It is the same word we saw in Romans 8:29 & 1 Peter 1:2. Surely this verse is not saying God merely foreknew what Jesus would choose do on the cross for that was no mere chance. Not a soul would deny that Christ coming to die on the cross for our salvation was a preplanned act of God that nothing could have changed. In turn, the word "foreknown" can only mean that God foreordained the action. God knew exactly what was going to happen because He ordained it before the foundation of the world. It is the exact same thing in the other two verses. God did not choose us based on a foreknowledge of what we would do. He had a foreknowledge of His ordination that took place before anything ever was. Arthur W. Pink has a wonderful quote regarding God's sovereign election:

A.W. Pink

> In the nature of things there cannot be anything known as what shall be, unless it is certain to be, and there is nothing certain to be unless God has ordained it shall be.[ii]

Even more than mere knowledge or even powerful ordination, the term "foreknowledge" speaks of a love like no other. Even in the beginning, we read of Adam knowing his wife (Genesis 4:1). In many cases, we see to know someone is often associated with intimacy. In much the same way, God's foreknowledge speaks of an intimate relationship that we are privileged enough to share with our loving Father. From eternity past, God had a special love for us.

Joel R. Beeke

> For God to truly know is for God to truly love. In Amos 3:2, God says to Israel, "You only have I known of all the families of the earth." That does not mean God was ignorant of what was happening in Babylon or Egypt. God knows everything in the world, including every sparrow that falls. But God's knowledge is inseparable from His special, paternal love to His chosen people...God's foreknowledge means that God has always been in love with His people. He has loved the elect from all eternity.[iii]

He had a foreknowledge of the intimate relationship He would come to have with every believer but, more importantly, He already had an intimate love for us even while we were yet enemies with him (Romans 5:8). Even more so, Romans 8:29 says he already knew us before anything ever was. That is how awesome our God is! Jeremiah 1:5 says, "Before I formed you in the womb I knew you," Our election is unconditional.

Charles H. Spurgeon

> I believe the doctrine of election, because I am quite sure that if God had not chosen me I would never have chosen him; and I am quite sure he chose me before I was born, or else he never would have chosen me afterward.[iv]

Were it conditional, all God would have seen in us is a condition of depravity; a condition of sinfulness that has no cure other than the blood of Christ which needs to be applied prior to us being healed.

Romans 9:16

So then it does not depend on the man who wills or the man who runs, but on God who has mercy.

Romans 10:20

I WAS FOUND BY THOSE WHO DID NOT SEEK ME,
I BECAME MANIFEST TO THOSE WHO DID NOT ASK FOR ME.

2 Timothy 1:9

who has saved us and called us with a holy calling, not according to our works, but according to His own purpose and grace which was granted us in Christ Jesus from all eternity,

John 15:16a

You did not choose Me but I chose you, and appointed you

Exodus 33:19

I will be gracious to whom I will be gracious, and will show compassion on whom I will show compassion.

Ephesians 1:5

He predestined us to adoption as sons through Jesus Christ to Himself, according to the kind intention of His will,

Acts 13:48

When the Gentiles heard this, they began rejoicing and glorifying the

> word of the Lord; and as many as had been appointed to eternal life believed.

By now, we should be able to clearly see that not only does God choose us but that He also does so based on His own purpose and will & not based on anything within ourselves or any foreknowledge of a choice we were to make.

1 Peter 2:8b-9

> for they stumble because they are disobedient to the word, and to this doom they were also appointed. But you are A CHOSEN RACE, A royal PRIESTHOOD, A HOLY NATION, A PEOPLE FOR God's OWN POSSESSION, so that you may proclaim the excellencies of Him who has called you out of darkness into His marvelous light;

God is always in control. Even those who claim God chose them still refuse to believe it fully for they feel the rest rejected of their own free will. The two are not mutually exclusive but rather mutually inclusive. We clearly see that the disobedient ones spoken of in 1 Peter 2:8 were only this way because they are appointed to that very doom; to wrath.

1 Thessalonians 5:9

> For God has not destined us for wrath, but for obtaining salvation through our Lord Jesus Christ,

Again, if He can appoint some to a doom of wrath, why can He not choose others to be saved? Isn't it obvious by now that God is in control? Isn't it obvious by now that God chooses who goes where? It is not saying God gives us the opportunity to choose Him. It does not say that God stands on the sidelines and hopes we choose Him (more on this in chapter 10). It says God has DESTINED us for obtaining salvation. He ordained us as His elect before the foundation of the world that we would be conformed to the image of His Son.

It is the last part that, as believers, we cannot forget. It is the main purpose behind election. God did not choose us so that we may boast in our position. He did not predestine us so that we could live however we wanted to live knowing that no choice of ours could ever change things anyway. All thoughts such as these should be pushed as far away from your mind as possible.

Ephesians 1:11 & 2:10

> also we have obtained an inheritance, having been predestined according to His purpose who works all things after the counsel of His will.......For we are His workmanship, created in Christ Jesus for good works, which God prepared beforehand so that we would walk in them.

Joel R. Beeke

> God wants to make His elect holy, for He has predestined them to be conformed to the image of His Son. No one can then say, "I am elect; therefore, I do not need to be Christlike." Rather, as Peter implies (in 1 Peter 1:2), a believer should say, "Because I am elect, I cannot avoid being Christlike."ᵛ

I would like to close out with another quote from Arthur W. Pink:

A.W. Pink

> If the Lord Jesus possesses all power in Heaven and earth then none can successfully resist His will. But it may be said, This is true in the abstract, nevertheless, Christ refuses to exercise this power, inasmuch as He will never force anyone to receive Him as their Lord and Saviour. In one sense that is true, but in another sense it is positively untrue. The salvation of any sinner is a matter of Divine power. By nature the sinner is at enmity with God, and naught but

Divine power operating within him can overcome this enmity; hence it is written, "No man can come unto Me, except the Father which hath sent Me draw him" (John 6:44). It is the Divine power overcoming the sinner's innate enmity which makes him willing to come to Christ that he might have life. But this "enmity" is not overcome in all-why? Is it because the enmity is too strong to be overcome? Are there some hearts so steeled against Him that Christ is unable to gain entrance? To answer in the affirmative is to deny His omnipotence. In the final analysis it is not a question of the sinner's willingness or unwillingness, for by nature all are unwilling. Willingness to come to Christ is the finished product of Divine power operating in the human heart and will in overcoming man's inherent and chronic "enmity," as it is written, "Thy people shall be willing in the day of Thy power" (Psa. 110:3). To say that Christ is unable to win to Himself those who are unwilling is to deny that all power in Heaven and earth is His. To say that Christ cannot put forth His power without destroying man's responsibility is a begging of the question here raised, for He has put forth His power and made willing those who have come to Him, and if He did this without destroying their responsibility, why "cannot" He do so with others? If He is able to win the heart of one sinner to Himself why not that of another? To say, as is usually said, the others will not let Him is to impeach His sufficiency. It is a question of His will. If the Lord Jesus has decreed, desired, purposed the salvation of all mankind, then the entire human race will be saved, or, otherwise, He lacks the power to make good His intentions; and in such a case it could never be said, "He shall see of the travail of His soul and be satisfied." The issue raised involves the deity of the Saviour, for a defeated Saviour cannot be God.[vi]

---

[i] Sam Storms, Chosen For Life: The Case for Divine Election [Crossway, 2007] pg. 22

[ii] Arthur W. Pink, The Sovereignty of God [Baker Books, 2004] pg. 109

[iii] Joel R. Beeke, Living for God's Glory: An Introduction to Calvinism [Reformation Trust Publishing, 2008] pg. 63

[iv] C.H. Spurgeon, C.H. Spurgeon's Autobiography, Volume 1 [Passmore and Alabaster, 1899] pg. 170

[v] Joel R. Beeke, Living for God's Glory: An Introduction to Calvinism [Reformation Trust Publishing, 2008] pg. 64

[vi] Arthur W. Pink, The Sovereignty of God [Baker Books, 2004] pp. 64-65

6 LIMITED ATONEMENT

Welcome to one of the most controversial topics within the Reformed Faith. It is one which has been the center of many an argument and debate. One might think the doctrine of election might be the most controversial but, as we covered, both sides typically believe in election of some sort even if they do not believe it to be unconditional. However, Limited Atonement cannot be explained away by some form of free will as it deals with something of certainty; either Christ certainly died for all or he did not. It can only be one of the two options. While each of the five points have their areas of difficulty in our modern age, this particular point is the one people tend to have the most difficulty with.

The reason for this is because of the simple fact that a false view of Christ has become the popular standard. How many times have you heard someone say, "God is love" In an effort to nullify His wrath? We love the idea of a loving God so much that we cannot bear to think of a God as being vengeful, wrathful, or jealous. Sure, we may admit He can feel these ways but, in their practical life, they will never stop to think about them. In their mind, God is love and that is that. There is no need to go any further. Now, if God is love, it stands to reason that Christ loves the entire world and everybody in it. At least, that would be the typical Arminian's view on John 3:16. Therefore, if Christ loves everybody, it also stands to reason that he died for everyone. After all, how can the Gospel call be sincere if he didn't even make a way for them with his blood? I hope to cover all these points in this chapter so that you, the reader, may better grasp the biblical doctrine of Limited Atonement.

John Murray

> On whose behalf did Christ offer himself a sacrifice? On whose behalf did he propitiate the wrath of God? Whom did he reconcile to God in the body of his flesh through death? Whom did he redeem from the curse of the law, from the guilt and power of sin, from the enthralling power and bondage of Satan? In whose stead and on whose behalf was he obedient unto death, even the death of the cross?[i]

If you already consider yourself a Calvinist, you are probably well aware of what we have gone over thus far. If you have never even heard of Calvinism, it would not surprise me if all of this seems a bit foreign to you. While it was the prevalent doctrinal standpoint of the Reformation and beyond, recent history has gone a very different direction to the point where Reformed doctrine is oftentimes viewed as evil, uncaring, and unloving. Please know this is not the case at all. Reformed doctrine is rooted in love, grace, and humility while exerting every effort to give all glory and praise to the Lord. It truly is unfortunate that Arminianism (in many shapes and forms) has become the leading form of Christianity among the many denominations. It seems so much hard work was put in over the centuries only to revert back into false doctrine. As it stands, most modern Christians hold Arminian views even if they have never heard of it by that title. While one reason is because it is what is taught in many churches in this present day and age, A.W. Pink puts it in another light that I feel says it best.

A.W. Pink

The reason why there is so little depth, so little intelligence, so little grasp of the fundamental verities of Christianity, is because so few believers have been established in the faith through hearing the doctrines of grace expounded, and through their own personal study of them.[ii]

A.W. Pink

The superficial work of many of the professional evangelists of the last fifty years is largely responsible for the erroneous views now current upon the bondage of the natural man, encouraged by the laziness of those in the pew in their failure to "prove all things".[iii]

It is my goal to rectify this. One of the biggest weaknesses in the pulpit today is the failure to correctly teach what took place on the cross. It is common to hear sermons declaring that Christ died for you and all you have to do is believe. The underlying belief here is that, while Christ already died for everyone, that individual must unlock the power through their belief. The atonement is merely waiting for the person to choose. This is the system of synergism that we briefly covered in chapter 3. However, as Joel R. Beeke states, "The death of Christ is not a provisional measure, but actually secures salvation; it does not just make sinners redeemable, but actually redeems."[iv]

The Five Points of Calvinism

Since not all men will be saved as the result of Christ's redeeming work, a limitation must be admitted. Either the atonement was limited in that it was designed to secure salvation for certain sinners, but not for others, or it was limited in that it was not intended to secure salvation for any, but was designed on to make it possible for God to pardon sinners on the condition that they believe. In other words, one must limit its design either in extent (it was not intended for all) or in effectiveness (it did not secure the salvation for any).[v]

What it really boils down to is where one chooses to place the limitation. Scripture is very clear that the limitation is not placed in the effectiveness. Scripture is also clear that Christ does not merely make a way for men to save themselves but actually does the saving.

Matthew 1:21

> She will bear a Son; and you shall call His name Jesus, for He will save His people from their sins.

Luke 19:10

> For the Son of Man has come to seek and to save that which is lost.

1 Timothy 1:15

> It is a trustworthy statement, deserving full acceptance, that Christ Jesus came into the world to save sinners, among whom I am foremost of all.

Galatians 1:3-4

> Grace to you and peace from God out Father and the Lord Jesus Christ, who gave Himself for our sins so that He might rescue us from this present evil age, according to the will of our God and Father.

If you remember from the previous chapter, John 8:44 says the unregenerate man is bound by the will of his father. It also says his father is the devil. Here in Galatians 1:3-4, we see Paul is writing to fellow Christians. These Christians now have a new Father; God. They are no longer under the will of the devil but are now under the will of God. Everything done is according to the will of the Father. Even the Son subjected to this will. How much more so do we? The will of our

Father is not that we would save ourselves after Christ made a way. The will of our Father is that Christ would rescue is; that he would save us.

Joel R. Beeke

Arminianism forgets that the atonement does not win God's love but is the provision of His love. In that provision, Christ paid the full price of justice. He did not make a down payment on the debt owed; He paid the full price of sin so that the Father as Judge could justly cancel the debt (Heb. 10:14-18).[vi]

Without a proper understanding of redemption, one will never truly grasp what Christ did for us. As Beeke points out, Christ did not merely make a down payment. He paid our debt in full. Redemption refers to a ransom. We were once in bondage to sin. We were owned by sin just as a slave was owned by his master. A slave had no free will of their own. He was the personal property of his master. If the price was right, he could sell a slave to another just as you might sell your car to a potential buyer. The only difference is that there was less paperwork involved in selling your slave.

For Christ to redeem us means that he purchased us in full. We have been bought with a price and transferred to the ownership of another Master. This was accomplished through the atoning blood. The blood bought us. The blood justified us. The blood sanctifies us. It is all in the power of the blood.

Charles Spurgeon

A redemption which pays a price, but does not ensure that which is purchased - a redemption which calls Christ a substitute for the sinner, but yet which allows the person to suffer - is altogether unworthy of our apprehensions of Almighty God.[vii]

To claim both that Christ died for us yet we have yet to unlock the power of his atonement is to say that he did nothing, was impotent, and that his work is essentially unfinished and incomplete. Furthermore, since we know many will go to Hell, to say Christ paid the price for them is to also say that God is a God of injustice.

Joel R. Beeke

> Arminianism does injustice to the basic biblical concept of redemption, which has its roots in the deliverance of the people of God out of Egypt. Redemption did not merely make their release from Egyptian bondage possible; it brought them out of bondage into the place of God's appointment Likewise, with propitiation, God's wrath is satisfied by the offering up of a sacrifice, and once His wrath is satisfied, it turns away. A ransom releases the one for whom it is paid. Therefore, the onus is on anyone who says that Christ's death did not actually secure the salvation of a defined group of people to show that his view does justice to these biblical terms. Arminianism does not do that. [viii]

Nowhere in all of Scripture have we seen God require a double payment. For God to condemn one to Hell even after Christ already paid the price in full is to say that God requires this double payment. It is to say that He was paid once by the blood yet still requires more as if He were some greedy mafia boss. This is absurd and is on the edge of heresy if not already embracing it full force.

Titus 2:14

> who gave Himself for us to redeem us from every lawless deed, and to purify for Himself a people for His own possession, zealous for good deeds.

Not only is it Christ doing the saving but he also does it with a purpose. He does not simply throw us a rope to climb out of the quicksand called sin. He actually crosses the quicksand, pulls us out, and ensures we will never fall back into it. How can we make such bold statements? It is because Titus 2:14 tells us Christ not only redeems us but that he also purifies us. He purifies us and makes us zealous for good deeds. It was not a good deed, us choosing Christ, that purified and saved; it was purification and salvation which caused us to desire to pursue good deeds.

While there is indeed a limitation within the atonement at some point, no one can ever claim this limitation has reduced the effectiveness of atonement. For the non-Elect, it is not effective at all as it was never meant to be. However, for the Elect, it is thoroughly effective and sufficient. It is the atonement that justified us.

Romans 3:24

> being justified as a gift by His grace through the redemption which is in Christ Jesus;

Romans 5:8-9

> But God demonstrates His own love toward us, in that while we were yet sinners, Christ died for us. Much more then, having now been justified by His blood, we shall be saved from the wrath of God through Him.

Colossians 1:13-14

> For He rescued us from the domain of darkness, and transferred us to the kingdom of His beloved Son, in whom we have redemption, the forgiveness of sins.

Christ not only rescues and justifies but he also sanctifies. As we saw in the last chapter, we are elected to be holy, sanctified, and set apart for God. Apart from this end purpose, our lives are empty with no meaning or reason for our election or even the atonement.

Hebrews 13:12

Therefore Jesus also, that He might sanctify the people through His own blood, suffered outside the gate.

Romans 8:30

and these whom He predestined, He also called; and these whom He called, He also justified; and these whom He justified, He also glorified.

1 Peter 1:20

But now having been freed from sin and enslaved to God, you derive your benefit, resulting in sanctification, and the outcome, eternal life.

1 Thessalonians 4:3a

For this is the will of God, your sanctification

There is a reason I wanted to recap a bit on unconditional election at the beginning of this chapter. It is because this doctrine really plays a big part in the limited atonement. We saw that God called His Elect before the foundation of the world. We also learned that this election was not based on anything within ourselves. It is this group and this group only that the limited atonement applies to.

John 10:14-18

"I am the good shepherd, and I know My own and My own know Me, even as the Father knows Me and I know the Father; and I lay down My life for the sheep. I have other sheep, which are not of this fold; I must bring them also, and they will hear My voice; and they will become one flock with one shepherd. For this reason the Father

> loves Me, because I lay down My life so that I may take it again. No one has taken it away from Me, but I lay it down on My own initiative I have authority to lay it down, and I have authority to take it up again This commandment I received from My Father."

John 10:24-29

> The Jews then gathered around Him, and were saying to Him, "How long will You keep us in suspense? If You are the Christ, tell us plainly." Jesus answered them, "I told you, and you do not believe; the works that I do in My Father's name, these testify of Me. But you do not believe because you are not of My sheep. My sheep hear My voice, and I know them, and they follow Me; and I give eternal life to them, and they will never perish; and no one will snatch them out of My hand. My Father, who has given them to Me, is greater than all; and no one is able to snatch them out of the Father's hand."

Christ did not die for every individual without exception. Not even in one instance was his death in vain. He died for his flock. He died for his sheep. In John 10, Christ says his sheep hear his voice. He says he knows his sheep. He says there are other sheep not currently in the fold and that he has plans to bring them in. Salvation and atonement are not at random. They both go hand in hand in a systematic manner. They go hand in hand with a purpose. The Son knows those whom the Father has given him and he intends to call each and every one of them into the fold without missing anybody.

John 17:9

> I ask on their behalf; I do not ask on behalf of the world, but of those whom You have given Me; for they are Yours;

Finally, to those who claim it is unfair for God to choose some yet condemn others, on what grounds do you lay your claim? Is it on any substantive biblical ground or is it merely pent up emotion that dissolves in water? As Augustus Stone has said, "We may praise God that He saves any than charge Him with injustice because He saves so few."

John Gerstner

> Why does God have any obligation to offer salvation to any sinner? Grace, by definition, is undeserved. If it were deserved, it would not be a gospel; it would not be grace. If it is a gospel of grace it must be undeserved. If it is undeserved how can it be said that God owes it to anyone?[ix]

As we covered in the beginning of the chapter, there are those who believe for a call to be universal and genuine, it must also necessitate Christ dying for all of these men so that they truly stand a fighting chance. However, this is only showing the fine ability to grasp at straws while neglecting the clear teachings of Scripture. Roger Nicole sums it up by saying, "the only requisite for a sincere invitation is this – that if the condition be fulfilled, that which is offered will actually be granted." Even Jesus himself said, "The one who comes to Me I will certainly not cast out" (John 6:37).

If one genuinely places their trust in Christ, that individual is saved. This is not because he or she can circumvent a limited atonement or unconditional election but because they fall in line with the two. Because of Total Depravity, we can know that no man will even choose to come to Christ apart from God's unconditional and merciful election combined with Christ's atonement for his sheep. The offer is universally placed on the table for any man to eat from. However, when man is left to his own bidding, he will never accept the call but will willingly reject it.

Keeping in line with the charge of unfairness, how does God handle those who have never had the opportunity to hear the Gospel? I'm sure we've all heard the analogy of an isolated tribe in Africa who has never heard the good news of Christ. If this tribe were to exist, would the members still be found guilty in God's court? Even if we agree with Nicole's statement regarding a sincere invitation, what do we make of those who have never even received the invitation?

John Gerstner

> Is it not unjust of God to damn a person who has had no opportunity to be saved? Why is it? Assuming that God does damn such persons, why is it unjust of Him to do so simply because they have no opportunity to be saved? If these persons are damned, they are damned because they are sinners; they are not damned because they have had the opportunity to be saved and have not utilized it. Their opportunity, or lack of it, has nothing to do with their being damned; they are damned because they are sinners.[x]

Just as with the previous charge of unfairness, this one is wrought with human emotion while being devoid of logic. A man is not condemned based on his ability to respond to the Gospel. He is not condemned based on what offers have come his way. No resident of Hell will ever be able to say he is there out of ignorance. He will only be able to say he is there because he was a wretched sinner who violated God's Law.

I'd like to close with a quote by Charles Spurgeon:

Charles H. Spurgeon

> We are often told that we limit the atonement of Christ, because we say that Christ has not made a satisfaction for all men, or all men would be saved. Now, our reply to this is, that, on the other hand, our opponents limit it: we do not. The Arminians say, Christ died for all men. Ask them what they mean by it. Did Christ die so as to secure the salvation of all men? They say, 'No, certainly not.' We ask them the next question – Did Christ die so as to secure the salvation of any man in particular? They answer, 'No.' They are obliged to admit this, if they are consistent. They say, 'No. Christ has died that any man may be saved if' – and then follow certain conditions of salvation. Now, who is it that limits the death of Christ? Why, you.

You say that Christ did not die so as infallibly to secure the salvation of anybody. We beg your pardon, when you say we limit Christ's death; we say, 'No, my dear sir, it is you that do it.' We say Christ so died that he infallibly secured the salvation of a multitude that no man can number, who through Christ's death not only may be saved, but are saved and cannot by any possibility run the hazard of being anything but saved. You are welcome to your atonement; you may keep it. We will never renounce ours for the sake of it.[xi]

---

[i] John Murray, Redemption: Accomplished and Applied [Wm. B. Eerdmans Publishing Company, 1955] pg. 76

[ii] Arthur W. Pink, The Sovereignty of God [Baker Books, 2004] pg. 214

[iii] ibid, pg. 140

[iv] Joel R. Beeke, Living for God's Glory: An Introduction to Calvinism [Reformation Trust Publishing, 2008] pg. 79

[v] The Five Points of Calvinism, pp. 40-41

[vi] Joel R. Beeke, Living for God's Glory: An Introduction to Calvinism [Reformation Trust Publishing, 2008] pg. 85

[vii] Charles Spurgeon, The Metropolitan Tabernacle Pulpit, Vol. XLIX, pg. 39

[viii] ibid, pg. 90

[ix] John Gerstner, Reasons For Faith [Soli Deo Gloria Publications, 1995] pg. 152

[x] Ibid, pg. 151

[xi] Cited by J.I. Packer, "Introductory Essay," in John Owen, The Death of Death in the Death of Christ [Banner of Truth, 1959] pg. 14

7 IRRESISTIBLE GRACE

God's grace: what does it mean? The topic of grace is anything but taboo. We hear pastors preach on it almost weekly. We hear evangelists throw the term around. We even sing songs about grace and how amazing it is. Despite this, if you were asked to define grace, how would you go about doing it? Is God's grace resistible? Surely, if men go to Hell, they must be resisting the grace of God, right? Wrong! As we covered in the previous chapter, God does not fail in His will to call people to Him as He does not call every person. In order to properly understand a Biblical view of grace, we must understand how it functions. As you have probably come to see by now, each point of TULIP builds on the previous; they stand and fall together. For one to claim to be a 3-point or 4-point Calvinist means, somewhere along the line, he is inconsistent. It isn't a game of JENGA where one or two blocks and safely be removed before the entire tower comes crashing down. Furthermore, each point really focuses on a single person in particular. Total Depravity focuses on the fallen nature of man. Unconditional Election focuses on the Father electing some to Himself out of His own grace and mercy. Limited Atonement focuses on the Son dying only for those whom the Father has given to him. Irresistible Grace focuses on the third Person of the Holy Trinity; the Holy Spirit. It focuses on the regenerating power of the Holy Spirit. Just as the

Father and Son do not fail in their parts, the Holy Spirit is equally as free of failure.

To one who does not properly understand depravity, election, or the power in the blood, he may come to the conclusion that he is free to choose or reject God as he will. There is nothing holding him down as far as he is concerned. Despite the common belief that the power to choose or reject lies with man, it is my goal to show what Scripture has to say about it; that the Holy Spirit never fails to regenerate those whom have been called by the Father and given to the Son. It is not on our timeline but rather, in His time.

I suppose the next logical step then is to define God's calling since everything else hangs on this precipice.

John 7:37

Now on the last day, the great day of the feast, Jesus stood and cried out, saying, "If anyone is thirsty, let him come to Me and drink."

Matthew 11:28

Come to Me, all who are weary and heavy-laden, and I will give you rest.

John 1:11-12

He came to His own, and those who were His own did not receive Him. But as many as received Him, to them He gave the right to become children of God, even to those who believe in His name,

John 3:16

For God so loved the world, that He gave His only begotten Son, that

> whoever believes in Him shall not perish, but have eternal life.

Revelation 3:20

> Behold, I stand at the door and knock; if anyone hears My voice and opens the door, I will come in to him and will dine with him, and he with Me.

Revelation 22:17

> The Spirit and the bride say, "Come " And let the one who hears say, "Come " And let the one who is thirsty come; let the one who wishes take the water of life without cost.

With verses like these, it is easy to see how one could conclude that man's salvation ultimately rests in his own hands. Even the beloved John 3:16 seems to point it out. However, the one thing we need to notice is that, while inviting people, it never says they will come. In fact, Scripture is quite clear that only the Elect will come.

This is because of the two different types of calls. The calling described above is the External Call. It is made without distinction to all who will hear. It is because of this fact that men are still found guilty in God's eyes. They have heard the call of the gospel but, just as many are called by it, many may also reject it (Hebrews 12:25). This is because it is outside our very nature to comply to it.

John 8:44a

> You are of your father the devil, and you want to do the desires of your father

The other type of call is Inward Call also known as the effectual Call. The effectual call is the only call that results in salvation (Acts

2:39). Without it, we would all perish since we have no good within ourselves.

Westminster Confession of Faith (10.1)

> All those whom God hath predestinated unto life, and those only, He is pleased, in His appointed and accepted time, effectually to call, by His Word and Spirit, out of that state of sin and death, in which they are by nature, to grace and salvation, by Jesus Christ; enlightening their minds spiritually and savingly to understand the things of God, taking away their heart of stone, and giving unto them a heart of flesh; renewing their wills, and by His almighty power, determining them to that which is good, and effectually drawing them to Jesus Christ: yet so, as they most freely, being made willing by His grace.

The Spirit no doubt has a role in salvation. The question is how much of a role do you believe He has? Is He watching and waiting as he casually prompts you to make the right decision or is he grabbing hold of you, giving you a complete makeover, and reshaping your very nature so that it will fall in line with God's plan for your life?

Romans 8:14

> For all who are being led by the Spirit of God, these are sons of God.

1 Corinthians 2:10-13

> For to us God revealed them through the Spirit; for the Spirit searches all things, even the depths of God. For who among men knows the thoughts of a man except the spirit of the man which is in him? Even so the thoughts of God no one knows except the Spirit of God. Now we have received, not the spirit of the world, but the Spirit who is from God, so that we may know the things freely given to us by God, which things we also speak, not in words taught by human wisdom, but in those taught by the Spirit, combining spiritual thoughts with spiritual words.

1 Corinthians 12:13

> Therefore I make known to you that no one speaking by the Spirit of God says, "Jesus is accursed"; and no one can say, "Jesus is Lord," except by the Holy Spirit.

All salvation comes through the Holy Spirit. Apart from the Spirit, there is no salvation. It is only through regeneration that one can have faith. It is only through becoming a new creature in Christ, that one can have faith.

2 Corinthians 5:17

> Therefore if anyone is in Christ, he is a new creature; the old things passed away; behold, new things have come.

Deuteronomy 30:6

> Moreover the LORD your God will circumcise your heart and the heart of your descendants, to love the LORD your God with all your heart and with all your soul, so that you may live.

Ezekiel 36:26-27

> Moreover, I will give you a new heart and put a new spirit within you; and I will remove the heart of stone from your flesh and give you a heart of flesh. I will put My Spirit within you and cause you to walk in My statutes, and you will be careful to observe My ordinances.

It is only by the Spirit that one can possibly know and understand the Word of God. This knowledge is not made known to everyone. Sure, everyone can hear and even understand to an extent but, pertaining to the eyes of the heart, they are blind. It may make sense on an elementary level but any further than that and it is foolishness (1

Corinthians 1:18). According to the solid truth of Scripture, it is only made known, tangible, and embraceable to God's Elect.

1 Corinthians 2:14

But a natural man does not accept the things of the Spirit of God, for they are foolishness to him; and he cannot understand them, because they are spiritually appraised.

Matthew 11:25-27

At that time Jesus said, "I praise You, Father, Lord of heaven and earth, that You have hidden these things from the wise and intelligent and have revealed them to infants. Yes, Father, for this way was well-pleasing in Your sight. All things have been handed over to Me by My Father; and no one knows the Son except the Father; nor does anyone know the Father except the Son, and anyone to whom the Son wills to reveal Him."

Luke 8:10

And He said, "To you it has been granted to know the mysteries of the kingdom of God, but to the rest it is in parables, so that SEEING THEY MAY NOT SEE, AND HEARING THEY MAY NOT UNDERSTAND.

Ephesians 1:17-18

that the God of our Lord Jesus Christ, the Father of glory, may give to you a spirit of wisdom and of revelation in the knowledge of Him. I pray that the eyes of your heart may be enlightened, so that you will know what is the hope of His calling, what are the riches of the glory of His inheritance in the saints,

As was stated earlier, there is an External Call and an Inward Call.

The Five Points of Calvinism

The gospel invitation extends a general outward call to salvation to all who hear the message. In addition to this external call, the Holy Spirit extends a special inward call to the Elect only. The general call can be, and often is, rejected, but the special call of the Spirit cannot be rejected; it always results in the conversion of those to whom it is made.[i]

Romans 1:6-7

among whom you also are the called of Jesus Christ; to all who are beloved of God in Rome, called as saints: Grace to you and peace from God our Father and the Lord Jesus Christ.

Romans 8:30

a and these whom He predestined, He also called; and these whom He called, He also justified; and these whom He justified, He also glorified.

In Romans 8:30, we see a distinction being made between the external call and the inward call. Obviously, not all who hear the Word are predestined, justified, and glorified. Only God's Elect, those who are inwardly called, can claim these things.

Romans 9:23-24

And He did so to make known the riches of His glory upon vessels of mercy, which He prepared beforehand for glory, even us, whom He also called, not from among Jews only, but also from among Gentiles.

Galatians 1:15-16

But when God, who had set me apart even from my mother's womb and called me through His grace, was pleased to reveal His Son in me so that I might preach Him among the Gentiles, I did not immediately consult with flesh and blood,

Ephesians 4:4

There is one body and one Spirit, just as also you were called in one hope of your calling;

2 Timothy 1:9

who has saved us and called us with a holy calling, not according to our works, but according to His own purpose and grace which was granted us in Christ Jesus from all eternity,

Hebrews 9:15

For this reason He is the mediator of a new covenant, so that, since a death has taken place for the redemption of the transgressions that were committed under the first covenant, those who have been called may receive the promise of the eternal inheritance.

1 Peter 1:15

but like the Holy One who called you, be holy yourselves also in all your behavior;

1 Peter 2:9

But you are A CHOSEN RACE, A royal PRIESTHOOD, A HOLY NATION, A PEOPLE FOR God's OWN POSSESSION, so that you may

> proclaim the excellencies of Him who has called you out of darkness
> into His marvelous light;

Again, God only calls inwardly those whom He has predestined before the foundation of the world. None who hear His inward call can resist it. The Spirit never fails in this call to bring the Elect to the Father through the Son. Everything is from God and succumbs to His sovereign will.

Isaiah 55:11

> So will My word be which goes forth from My mouth;
> It will not return to Me empty,
> Without accomplishing what I desire,
> And without succeeding in the matter for which I sent it.

John 3:27

> John answered and said, "A man can receive nothing unless it has
> been given him from heaven.

While Irresistible Grace is a Biblical doctrine, it has led to many erroneous beliefs over the years. Many of the false beliefs stem from a lack of understanding of the Five Points of Calvinism. A proper Biblical understanding does nothing more than take grace and boasting from ourselves and redirects it to its appropriate Subject: God. It helps us to understand the sovereignty of God. One of the most dangerous false beliefs that has stemmed from the ignorant is fatalism. Fatalism is "The false belief that since all events are predetermined by God, man should do nothing because his actions will not be of any consequence". This is in direct violation of Scripture.

1 Peter 1:15

> but like the Holy One who called you, be holy yourselves also in all your behavior;

Matthew 28:19

> Go therefore and make disciples of all the nations, baptizing them in the name of the Father and the Son and the Holy Spirit,

Why should one continue to give the external call to those around him even if it already decreed who will believe and who won't? Why should one even try if everything is done by God and nothing lies within man in and of himself? Why should one even try to live a holy life if God has declared him justified? The answer is simple: BECAUSE GOD HAS COMMANDED IT. What greater reason does one need?

---

[i] The Five Points of Calvinism: Defined, Defended, Documented [Presbyterian & Reformed Pub Co] pg. 61

8 PERSEVERANCE OF THE SAINTS

Up to this point, we have reviewed four of the five points. We learned that it is by the changed nature of a man that he desires God. Because the very nature of man changes, his very desires change as well. It is in these changed desires that one now feels irresistibly drawn to God. In this chapter, we will be going over the final point; the perseverance of the saints. We have gone over a lot of information that is very difficult to limit to merely five chapters of a single book. We've learned that we are totally depraved human beings incapable of choosing God. We've learned that God chose us out of His own mercy and grace and not based on a foreseen choice we would make. We've learned that Christ did not die for every person but rather, for those whom the Father had given him before the foundation of the world. We've learned that once God calls us, it is irresistible and everything in our newly changed nature screams to cling to Him. We will wrap up the series with such a confidence in our salvation that we might know it is eternal.

While the first four points have come under much scrutiny and have been very strong areas of contention, it is this last point which is seemingly more accepted among Protestant denominations. In fact, while many Baptists have a hard time accepting TULI, they cling to Perseverance of the Saints and teach it proudly. That being said, there are still many who reject the doctrine. At some point, most people will question their salvation. This is a natural human response to various circumstances. Some will answer this question by realizing the truth of Scripture. Sadly, there are many who will come to the conclusion that they have lost their salvation, nobody is really secure, and we are all just trying our hardest to stay saved.

Scripture teaches that we have freedom in Christ. What good is this freedom if there is a chance of losing it at every turn? Scripture teaches a peace of God. Where is the peace when we are constantly worried of falling away? Faith is a gift from God. It is not something we earn. It is not something we work for. God gave it to us in grace. Through His gift, we have assurance of hope.

Westminster Confession of Faith

> They, whom God hath accepted in His Beloved, effectually called, and sanctified by His Spirit, can neither totally nor finally fall away from the state of grace, but shall certainly persevere therein to the end, and be eternally saved.

Loraine Boettner

> This doctrine does not stand alone but is a necessary part of the Calvinistic system of theology. The doctrines of Election and Efficacious Grace logically imply the certain salvation of those who receive these blessings. If God has chosen men absolutely and unconditionally to eternal life, and if His Spirit effectively applies to them the benefits of redemption, the inescapable conclusion is that these persons shall be saved.[i]

Scripture makes it very clear that not every person who claims to have faith is actually a believer.

John 7:37

> Not everyone who says to Me, 'Lord, Lord,' will enter the kingdom of heaven

This is not saying that God excludes certain people of faith. It is saying not everyone who claims to have faith actually does. There are many people who know all about God but do not actually KNOW God. Jesus taught on the subject of people who claimed to be believers but later fell away. He used the parable of the sower.

Matthew 13:3-8

> And He spoke many things to them in parables, saying, "Behold, the sower went out to sow; and as he sowed, some seeds fell beside the road, and the birds came and ate them up. Others fell on the rocky places, where they did not have much soil; and immediately they sprang up, because they had no depth of soil. But when the sun had risen, they were scorched; and because they had no root, they withered away. Others fell among the thorns, and the thorns came up and choked them out. And others fell on the good soil and yielded a crop, some a hundredfold, some sixty, and some thirty.

Without going too far off the beaten path, I feel it is important to have an understanding of this passage at least on a basic level. We see Jesus referring to four types of seed. Due to his explanation in the following verses of the passage, we can see how it all ties into the doctrine of Perseverance of the Saints.

The first type of seed we see is that which fell beside the road. This seed represents those who hear the Word but lack understanding. It falls on deaf ears so to speak. As a result, it is taken away by the birds and is of no benefit to the person who heard it.

The second type of seed is that which fell on rocky places and was dried up by the sun. This represents the person who has heard the word and taken it in but does not have any roots. He has tossed it around in his mind and might even be convinced logically of its truth but, in the end, it is not rooted in Christ through the Spirit. As a result, it is not fed with Life and will eventually wither and die.

The third type is that which begins to grow but is soon choked out by thorns. This represents the person who hears the word, appears to be changed by it, and even begins to grow. How many new Christians do we know who are currently in this state? Do you know anybody who has recently professed his faith in Christ and has started to sprout the fruit of said faith? It is this third type of seed that has perhaps led many to believe that salvation can be lost. The reason for this is because, as we can see in the passage, it is eventually choked out by the thorns only to die in the end. Be it the burdens of life, the temptations of the world, or any number of external factors, this person eventually succumbs to them and his faith is no more. While we hope and pray these individuals will continue in the faith and grow into solid Christians, the fact of the matter is that some will seem to hit a brick wall only to reject the very One they were just professing. Is this genuine evidence of forfeited salvation? Christ Himself has said this is not the case.

Matthew 7:21-23

"Not everyone who says to Me, 'Lord, Lord,' will enter the kingdom of heaven, but he who does the will of My Father who is in heaven will enter. "Many will say to Me on that day, 'Lord, Lord, did we not prophesy in Your name, and in Your name cast out demons, and in Your name perform many miracles?' "And then I will declare to them, 'I never knew you; DEPART FROM ME, YOU WHO PRACTICE LAWLESSNESS.'

John 2:19

They went out from us, but they were not really of us; for if they had been of us, they would have remained with us; but they went

> out, so that it would be shown that they all are not of us.

Many people claim to be Christians. Many people actually feel they are Christians. Unfortunately, they do not understand what it means to be a Christian. It is not a title to be claimed. It is not something we can work for. It is a change of nature which only God can perform. Only those who have received His gift of faith are saved.

This brings us to the fourth type of seed: that which lands in good soil and produces fruit. This person does not merely sprout leaves. He flourishes and produces wonderful fruit many times over. He represents the mature Christian who has the Spirit working within. He trusts in his Savior and knows that, while his salvation is secure, he has a duty to his Lord. He has a Father to obey and a Master to serve.

Of the four types of seed, only one was a true believer with true saving faith. The others were only on a superficial level if even that much. If one falls away from faith, he was as the seed that fell by the roadside, rocky places, or thorns. He never truly had saving faith. The person with true saving faith will abide with God forever.

God has given the promise of eternal security in Him. We do not have to live in fear of losing our salvation. If we are confident in our love for God and our faith in Christ, our salvation will always remain for we will always abide in Him.

Ephesians 1:13-14

> In Him, you also, after listening to the message of truth, the gospel of your salvation—having also believed, you were sealed in Him with the Holy Spirit of promise, who is given as a pledge of our inheritance, with a view of redemption of God's own possession, to the praise of His glory.

Philippians 1:6

> For I am confident of this very thing, that He who began a good
> work in you will perfect it until the day of Christ Jesus.

Matthew 18:12-14

> What do you think? If any man has a hundred sheep, and one of
> them has gone astray, does he not leave the ninety-nine on the
> mountains and go and search for the one that is straying? If it turns
> out that he finds it, truly I say to you, he rejoices over it more than
> over the ninety-nine which have not gone astray. So it is not the will
> of your Father who is in heaven that one of these little ones perish.

In order to properly understand what Jesus was saying in that last
passage, one must understand the relationship between a shepherd and
his sheep. The shepherd was solely responsible for the wellbeing of the
sheep. Sheep are dumb and would often wander astray. When they
were away from the herd, they were susceptible to danger. The
shepherd would then go out and look for the sheep. In the same way,
when a Christian goes astray, we can be assured he will be brought
back into the fold. How do we know, it is because Scripture tells us
that it is not the will of the Father for any of His sheep to perish. He
keeps us secure in Christ. This is a promise of Scripture!

John 5:24

> Truly, truly, I say to you, he who hears My word, and believes Him
> who sent Me, has eternal life, and does not come into judgment, but
> has passed out of death into life.

Notice how it speaks in the past tense. It does not say one will
pass from death into life at some later point. It says, if one has faith,
they have already passed from death into life. They completely bypass
the judgment because they are in Christ. If one has already passed from

death into life, how can they possibly fall back into death again? The old self is dead forever. The eternal life starts at the moment of salvation and it can never be lost.

Once you have the gift of faith, God sets out to work in perfecting you through sanctification, justification, and glorification. God gives His promise that He will continue to do this until Christ's return. He does not say He will continue it until one falls away.

Romans 8:28-39

> And we know that God causes all things to work together for good to those who love God, to those who are called according to His purpose. For those whom He foreknew, He also predestined to become conformed to the image of His Son, so that He would be the firstborn among many brethren; and these whom He predestined, He also called; and these whom He called, He also justified; and these whom He justified, He also glorified. What then shall we say to these things? If God is for us, who is against us? He who did not spare His own Son, but delivered Him over for us all, how will He not also with Him freely give us all things? Who will bring a charge against God's elect? God is the one who justifies; who is the one who condemns? Christ Jesus is He who died, yes, rather who was raised, who is at the right hand of God, who also intercedes for us. Who will separate us from the love of Christ? Will tribulation, or distress, or persecution, or famine, or nakedness, or peril, or sword? Just as it is written,
> "FOR YOUR SAKE WE ARE BEING PUT TO DEATH ALL DAY LONG;
> WE WERE CONSIDERED AS SHEEP TO BE SLAUGHTERED."
> But in all these things we overwhelmingly conquer through Him who loved us. For I am convinced that neither death, nor life, nor angels, nor principalities, nor things present, nor things to come, nor powers, nor height, nor depth, nor any other created thing, will be able to separate us from the love of God, which is in Christ Jesus our Lord.

This is a great passage that drives home the doctrine of Perseverance of the Saints. First and foremost, it speaks of God's purpose. While many will admit God can, and often does, intervene in impersonal issues, this passage goes much deeper. It speaks of God's purpose in the life of individuals. It speaks of His calling and our security. This security is not based on some impersonal deity. It isn't even based on our own doing. It is based solely in God's sovereignty through the love of Christ. There is nothing that can separate us from this love. It is a point that Paul goes to great measure to stress.

Do not be deceived into thinking you can act any way you want because of your eternal security. As I covered in my last book, we are not to use grace as a covering for evil. Furthermore, Scripture tells us how one of true faith will act.

1 John 2:4

> The one who says, "I have come to know Him," and does not keep His commandments, is a liar, and the truth is not in him;

Notice it does not call the man a liar about saying he is currently with God. It calls him a liar by saying he never even came to know God at all. This is not speaking of following every single commandment of God. Obviously, we all sin. This is why we need a Savior. I can guarantee you that I came to know God many years ago and He has been perfecting me ever since. If I were perfect already, He would have no need to perfect me. No, this verse speaking of one who is still in his old nature, does not struggle with sin, yet claims Christ as Savior.

1 Corinthians 6:9b-11

> Do not be deceived; neither fornicators, nor idolaters, nor adulterers, nor effeminate, nor homosexuals, nor thieves, nor the covetous, nor drunkards, nor revilers, nor swindlers, will inherit the kingdom of God. Such were some of you; but you were washed, but you were sanctified, but you were justified in the name of the Lord Jesus Christ and in the Spirit of our God.

Though our justification is complete, we are a long way from perfected. From the moment of our salvation, the process of sanctification begins. Our old nature dies and a new one is born. We continually work out our salvation with fear and trembling (Philippians 2:12). Thankfully, God has promised to complete the good work He began in us (Philippians 1:6). We share in the resurrection of Christ.

Romans 5:1-5

Therefore, having been justified by faith, we have peace with God through our Lord Jesus Christ, through whom also we have obtained our introduction by faith into this grace in which we stand; and we exult in hope of the glory of God. And not only this, but we also exult in our tribulations, knowing that tribulation brings about perseverance; and perseverance, proven character; and proven character, hope; and hope does not disappoint, because the love of God has been poured out within our hearts through the Holy Spirit who was given to us.

Consider various trials and tribulations to be a blessing. They give us an opportunity to trust God but they also serve another purpose. Just as the Old Testament law pointed out the sin in man, trials and tribulations give glory to God by pointing out the promise of perseverance of the saints.

1 Thessalonians 5:23

Now may the God of peace Himself sanctify you entirely; and may your spirit and soul and body be preserved complete, without blame at the coming of our Lord Jesus Christ.

John 10:27-30

"My sheep hear My voice, and I know them, and they follow Me; and I give eternal life to them, and they will never perish; and no one will snatch them out of My hand. "My Father, who has given them to

Me, is greater than all; and no one is able to snatch them out of the Father's hand. "I and the Father are one."

John 6:39

This is the will of Him who sent Me, that of all that He has given Me I lose nothing, but raise it up on the last day.

1 Peter 1:4-5

to obtain an inheritance which is imperishable and undefiled and will not fade away, reserved in heaven for you, who are protected by the power of God through faith for a salvation ready to be revealed in the last time.

God protects our salvation. He has promised it. It is His Will that Jesus should lose nothing he has been given. That includes us. God has us and it is impossible for us to be snatched out of His hand. Our inheritance is eternally reserved for us.

2 Peter 1:10

Therefore, brethren, be all the more diligent to make certain about His calling and choosing you; for as long as you practice these things, you will never stumble;

2 Timothy 4:18

The Lord will rescue me from every evil deed, and will bring me safely to His heavenly kingdom; to Him be the glory forever and ever. Amen.

Check your faith daily. Ensure you are walking with the Lord and not deceiving yourself as many already are doing. If you are confident in your salvation and your relationship with the Lord, be at peace in knowing you will persevere until the final day when Christ lifts you up and God perfects the work within you. Nothing can change this fact!

---

[i] Loraine Boettner, Reformed Doctrine of Predestination [1936] pg. 182

Part Three
In Full Bloom

Travis W. Rogers

9 PROCEED WITH CAUTION

Over the course of this book, we have gone through some of the major differences between Roman Catholicism and Protestantism. We covered much of the teachings of the Catholic Church by using their own writings and then compared them to Scripture. The undeniable conclusion is that there are many irreconcilable differences and that the Catholic Church is to be viewed as the mission field in desperate need of the Gospel and teaching of the doctrines of grace. Now, we are going to move away from this area in particular and cover a much broader subject. That subject is the danger of false teaching and the importance of sound Biblical doctrine.

1 Timothy 3:16

By common confession, great is the mystery of godliness:
He who was revealed in the flesh,
Was vindicated in the Spirit,
Seen by angels,
Proclaimed among the nations,
Believed on in the world,
Taken up in glory.

1 Timothy 4:1

> But the Spirit explicitly says that in later times some will fall away from the faith, paying attention to deceitful spirits and doctrines of demons,

Our faith is based on Christ and the Word of God alone. Despite this, there are many out there who deny it. Not only are there other religions but there are also those who claim the title of Christianity yet teach something that Scripture refers to as "doctrines of demons." To get a better idea as to what these doctrines of demons are, we are going to see what Paul had to say to Timothy on the matter.

1 Timothy 4:2

> by means of the hypocrisy of liars seared in their own conscience as with a branding iron,

Those who teach doctrines of demons do so without conviction. They believe their own lies. They have given in to the demonic influence and lies of Satan to the point where they no longer see the line between truth and heresy. It was my intent to vividly paint this picture in the first couple chapters. We covered the irreconcilable differences between Catholics and Protestants such as works versus grace, the priesthood, the Mass, the re-sacrificing of Christ over and over again, penance & indulgences, as well as others. These are all false doctrines that fly in the face of Scripture but use the Traditions of the Roman Catholic Church to support themselves. I was kind in calling them false doctrines. Scripture is not so kind.

1 Timothy 4:3

> men who forbid marriage and advocate abstaining from foods which God has created to be gratefully shared in by those who believe and know the truth.

Both of these are doctrines that the Catholic Church holds near and dear. Priests are not allowed to marry. Of course, this was not always the case. The Roman Catholic priesthood was once allowed to marry without issue. Unfortunately, this wonderful blessing and covenant with God was not to last. At the First Lateran Council of 1123, rules were imposed barring unmarried priests from marrying but allowing already married priests to remain married. Of course, it didn't take long for that to change. Another rule was imposed, in the Second Lateran Council of 1139, forcing married priests to leave their wives which caused many of them to be cast out and become street walking prostitutes just so they could survive. For those who chose to continue having sexual relations with their wife, they were viewed as fornicators and were not privy to receive any of the benefits of the Church. As if this wasn't bad enough, even the children were to suffer as they were declared illegitimate. This resulted in their being ineligible to enter the clergy or, for many of them, to even be married themselves once they reached adulthood.[i] This is all the grim history surrounding the Roman Catholic Church. Why would they forbid marriage? Even Peter was married and he is the one they claim to be their first Pope.

Along the same lines, the Roman Catholic Church also teaches that you cannot eat meat on Fridays. Granted, this is most commonly enforced only during Lent, there are still many Catholic Churches that have extended this practice to include every Friday of the year. According to Catholic teaching, eating meat on a Friday during Lent is considered to be a mortal sin.

So, I state it again:

1 Timothy 4:1&3

> But the Spirit explicitly says that in later times some will fall away from the faith, paying attention to deceitful spirits and doctrines of demons,..........men who forbid marriage and advocate abstaining from foods[which God has created to be gratefully shared in by those who believe and know the truth.

As I said, Scripture is not so kind. It specifically calls these teachings of the Catholic Church to be doctrines of demons. They are lies straight from the pits of Hell as are the other doctrines we covered in the first two chapters. Again, this is not an attack on Catholics but it is indeed a brutal attack on the religion that has perverted the Gospel and doctrines of grace in favor of a doctrine of legalism and tradition of men. Some say I am too harsh. I say I am not harsh enough. There is a very real danger in false teaching. It was the very first verse I quoted:

1 Timothy 4:1

> But the Spirit explicitly says that in later times some will fall away from the faith, paying attention to deceitful spirits and doctrines of demons,

We are called to draw people to Christ, not to draw them away from Him. False teachers present a very real danger to the Church body.

Matthew 24:4-5

> And Jesus answered and said to them, "See to it that no one misleads you. For many will come in My name, saying, 'I am the Christ,' and will mislead many."

Acts 20:29

> I know that after my departure savage wolves will come in among you, not sparing the flock; and from among your own selves men will arise, speaking perverse things, to draw away the disciples after them.

False teachers are compared to a pack of savage wolves that tear apart the Church body and do not spare anybody.

2 Thessalonians 2:3-4

> Let no one in any way deceive you, for it will not come unless the apostasy comes first, and the man of lawlessness is revealed, the son of destruction, who opposes and exalts himself above every so-called god or object of worship, so that he takes his seat in the temple of God, displaying himself as being God.

That one sounds a lot like the Pope doesn't it? Sitting high on the throne, making people kiss his ring, taking on the title "Vicar of Christ" which literally means one who acts as a substitute. The Pope has taken on the title of a substitute Christ. One can't display themselves as God any more than this even if they tried.

2 Thessalonians 2:10

> and with all the deception of wickedness for those who perish, because they did not receive the love of the truth so as to be saved.

1 John 2:18

> Children, it is the last hour; and just as you heard that antichrist is coming, even now many antichrists have appeared; from this we know that it is the last hour.

The fact that false teaching is such a danger makes the need for Godly teachers all the greater. Teachers have a very high calling and an even higher responsibility to teach the Truth with accuracy.

James 3:1

> Let not many of you become teachers, my brethren, knowing that as such we will incur a stricter judgment.

1 Timothy 4:6

> In pointing out these things to the brethren, you will be a good servant of Christ Jesus, constantly nourished on the words of the faith and of the sound doctrine which you have been following.

True teachers are always feeding on the Word of God. We are always diving head first into Scripture in order to gain a better understanding of the Truth. We act as the Bereans:

Acts 17:11

> Now these were more noble-minded than those in Thessalonica, for they received the word with great eagerness, examining the Scriptures daily to see whether these things were so.

2 Timothy 3:16-17

> All Scripture is inspired by God and profitable for teaching, for reproof, for correction, for training in righteousness; so that the man of God may be adequate, equipped for every good work.

Scripture is the only true litmus test. If it is not found in Scripture, it is to be rejected. If something contrary or in addition to Scripture is taught, the teacher is to be rejected and shunned. Scripture is what equips us for every good work. It is what makes us adequate. Its purpose is for teaching, reproof, correction, and training in righteousness. Sola Scriptura! By Scripture Alone!

Scripture is plain that, while not everyone is to desire to be a teacher in the official sense, all are called to teach truth as fellow believers in Christ (Hebrews 5:12-14). We are all called to search the Scriptures daily. In fact, this is what John tells us all to do in order to know the Truth.

1 John 4:1-3

Beloved, do not believe every spirit, but test the spirits to see whether they are from God, because many false prophets have gone out into the world. By this you know the Spirit of God: every spirit that confesses that Jesus Christ has come in the flesh is from God; and every spirit that does not confess Jesus is not from God; this is the spirit of the antichrist, of which you have heard that it is coming, and now it is already in the world.

The first place we should start in testing the spirits is to see what their basic teaching is regarding Jesus. Do they teach of him being 100% man while also being 100% God or do they teach something contrary. Peter says if they confess Christ is God in the flesh, that teacher is from God. However, we must realize that there are many other perversions. One can easily claim Jesus was man and God yet then detract from who he really was by diminishing his role. Again, the Catholic Church does this repeatedly by diminishing the doctrines of grace and refusing to accept that Christ died once for all through their re-sacrifice over and over again during the Mass. This only reinforces the importance of knowing Scripture and being able to recall them during those crucial moments. This can only be done by daily examination and study.

1 John 4:5-6

They are from the world; therefore they speak as from the world, and the world listens to them. We are from God; he who knows God listens to us; he who is not from God does not listen to us By this we know the spirit of truth and the spirit of error.

The spirit of Truth will teach from the Word of God. The spirit of error will reject the Word of God by either adding to it or detracting from it. Scripture tells us what will become of this man:

Revelation 22:18-19

> I testify to everyone who hears the words of the prophecy of this book: if anyone adds to them, God will add to him the plagues which are written in this book; and if anyone takes away from the words of the book of this prophecy, God will take away his part from the tree of life and from the holy city, which are written in this book.

As a teacher, I am held to a very high standard and I do my best to ensure the accuracy of what I teach.

1 Timothy 4:16

> Pay close attention to yourself and to your teaching; persevere in these things, for as you do this you will ensure salvation both for yourself and for those who hear you.

---

[i] James A. Brundage, Law, Sex, and Christian Society in Medieval Europe [1987] pg. 220

10 MAIN CHARACTER OR SUPPORTING CAST?

While the vast majority of this book has been spent expounding on the doctrines of grace, the underlying theme has been the danger of false teaching. In fact, it is because of this false teaching that we have such a strong need for sound Biblical teaching. As we come to a close, we are going to cover an even greater subject. It is the subject of salvation. Even more detailed, it is the subject of how much of a part God plays in it. Is He the main character in this play or is He just a supporting cast member who cheers us on in our quest for eternity? You may recognize much of the content of this chapter from what you just read earlier. I believe it is important to rehash some of the points for the purpose of adequately driving home the overall message. My hope is that by the end of the chapter, you will know with certainty who the Composer really is.

The answer really is a simple one. God is not only the Composer but He also orchestrates the entire play. He came up with the concept, wrote the script, designed the set, directed the show, and closed out the credits with two words: JESUS CHRIST!

John MacArthur

Who is responsible for individual salvation – God or the person? Put

> another way, "Did God sovereignly elect us and save us? Or did He act in accord with what He knew we would do?" In other words, "Who makes the first move?"[i]

There are many today who place God at the forefront in their speech yet their doctrine reflects otherwise. Many say God is in control of all things yet then yield this control in favor of their own control. These people make the claims that God calls and makes possible salvation but we must do the rest of the job on our own in order to make anything legitimate. Sadly, this is not what Scripture teaches.

1 Corinthians 1:30

> But by His doing you are in Christ Jesus, who became to us wisdom from God, and righteousness and sanctification, and redemption,

It is by God's doing and by God's doing alone. We are going to cover some of these areas from a Scriptural standpoint throughout these final pages to see what it is exactly that God does while orchestrating His plan that came from eternity.

1 Peter 1:1a&2a

> Peter, an apostle of Jesus Christ, To those who reside as aliens,............who are chosen according to the foreknowledge of God the Father,

There are some out there who teach that God chooses people based on His foreknowledge of what they would choose of their own doing. In other words, they believe God makes salvation possible but then leaves it up to the individual person to accept it or reject it. They agree that there is an Elect but they say this election was based on the free will choice of the individual. In other words, God looked into the future, saw the choice man would make, and then elected him to be one of His own down the road in His own good timing. With this school of thought, it gives man something to boast about. It says that man made a righteous choice; man accepted a universal offer, man stepped up to God, and man essentially saved himself. It is compelled to teach that God does not save but only makes a way to save. Either that or it must say that God does the saving but only if we allow Him to which places us over God in the sense that we start telling Him what is acceptable and what is not. Furthermore, if salvation is only based upon God's foreknowledge of the choice of man, where did the saving faith come from to begin with? It certainly wouldn't have been initiated by God if He is only reacting instead of initiating. This is clearly not the Truth.

Romans 8:7

because the mind set on the flesh is hostile toward God; for it does not subject itself to the law of God, for it is not even able to do so,

Ephesians 2:3

Among them we too all formerly lived in the lusts of our flesh, indulging the desires of the flesh and of the mind, and were by nature children of wrath, even as the rest.

Colossians 1:21

And although you were formerly alienated and hostile in mind, engaged in evil deeds,

1 Corinthians 2:14

But a natural man does not accept the things of the Spirit of God, for they are foolishness to him; and he cannot understand them, because they are spiritually appraised.

As the Scriptures point out, there is nothing in us that would ever choose God. Before salvation, we were hostile toward God. We were children of wrath. We saw the things of God as foolishness. In essence, we hated God and had no desire to turn to Him. Even if we didn't consciously hate God, our actions proved otherwise. We were at war with God and most of us didn't even know it. Therefore, we know God's foreknowledge was not of an action we would make as the only possible action we could have made was to continue rejecting Him. As a result, we must continue to look and see what the true context of "foreknowledge" really is.

Romans 8:29-30

> For those whom He foreknew, He also predestined to become conformed to the image of His Son, so that He would be the firstborn among many brethren; and these whom He predestined, He also called; and these whom He called, He also justified; and these whom He justified, He also glorified.

We see here that everyone whom God foreknew, He also predestined. By itself, one might be able to argue that salvation is based upon God's foreknowledge of a choice. However, that is the problem. It is a doctrine that stands alone. When used in context with other Scripture, we see an entirely different meaning. The word used for "foreknew" is the Greek word *proginosko* which simply means to know in advance. However, the Greek word used for predestined is *proorizo* which means to ordain in advance. Did God simply ordain something that He saw in the beginning? Again, this is impossible because, as pointed out in the above verses, every part of our being was against God.

Acts 2:23

> this Man, delivered over by the predetermined plan and foreknowledge of God, you nailed to a cross by the hands of godless

men and put Him to death.

Everything hinges on the election of God; His predetermined plan. All Scripture is saying is that God had full knowledge of what was going on. God is omniscient. He knows all things. He was well aware of the plan He was setting in place. He knew it in advance because He ordained it in advance. The two phrases go hand in hand and actually share the same interpretation of each other.

1 Peter 1:20

For He was foreknown before the foundation of the world, but has appeared in these last times for the sake of you

Notice Scripture says that Jesus was foreknown before the foundation of the world. If we follow the same school of thought that many people do, we would be forced to say that this passage means nothing more than Jesus was known by God in advance. However, we know that there is much more to the meaning of this phrase.

Jeremiah 1:5a

Before I formed you in the womb I knew you,

John 10:14

I am the good shepherd, and I know My own and My own know Me,

God did not merely know the Son in advance. He ordained what would happen in advance. We also see that Jesus knows his own in an intimate way that goes beyond the normal bounds of general knowledge. The same is said in Jeremiah where it speaks of foreknowledge on an intimate level before even being in the womb. In other words, those whom God foreknew on an intimate level in advance, He also predestined.

Romans 11:2

> God has not rejected His people whom He foreknew Or do you not know what the Scripture says in the passage about Elijah, how he pleads with God against Israel?

Notice it says nothing about God foreknowing a choice. It specifically speaks of God foreknowing the individual. Of course, God knows every person inside and out so it cannot be speaking of a general knowledge. It is differentiating this by referring to the intimate knowledge that God foreknew of His Elect before the foundation of the world when He ordained His plan. This concept is also found in Romans 9.

Romans 9:23

> And He did so to make known the riches of His glory upon vessels of mercy, which He prepared beforehand for glory,

Romans 9:15-16 & 18

> For He says to Moses, "I WILL HAVE MERCY ON WHOM I HAVE MERCY, AND I WILL HAVE COMPASSION ON WHOM I HAVE COMPASSION." So then it does not depend on the man who wills or the man who runs, but on God who has mercy......... So then He has mercy on whom He desires, and He hardens whom He desires.

God prepared His Elect beforehand in order that we could share in His glory through an intimate relationship with Him as the Father. All of this was from Him and our own choices had no bearing on anything because our choice was bound by our nature of wrath.

Now that we have clarified the proper relationship between God's foreknowledge and His predestined plan, let's go back to the beginning and move on from there.

1 Corinthians 1:30

> But by His doing you are in Christ Jesus, who became to us wisdom from God, and righteousness and sanctification, and redemption,

Every single part of salvation is accredited to God. We are going to touch on a few of the actions God initiates and completes regarding the plan on salvation.

GOD WILLS

John 1:12-13

> But as many as received Him, to them He gave the right to become children of God, even to those who believe in His name, who were born, not of blood nor of the will of the flesh nor of the will of man, but of God.

Ephesians 1:5&11

> He predestined us to adoption as sons through Jesus Christ to Himself, according to the kind intention of His will,......also we have obtained an inheritance, having been predestined according to His purpose who works all things after the counsel of His will,

Nothing is outside the will of God. The only reason we have salvation is because God willed it in the beginning. He ordained it to be so.

GOD DRAWS

John 6:44

No one can come to Me unless the Father who sent Me draws him; and I will raise him up on the last day.

GOD GRANTS

John 6:65

And He was saying, "For this reason I have said to you, that no one can come to Me unless it has been granted him from the Father."

GOD CALLS

1 Thessalonians 2:12

so that you would walk in a manner worthy of the God who calls you into His own kingdom and glory.

2 Thessalonians 2:14

It was for this He called you through our gospel, that you may gain the glory of our Lord Jesus Christ.

1 Timothy 1:9

who has saved us and called us with a holy calling, not according to our works, but according to His own purpose and grace which was granted us in Christ Jesus from all eternity,

1 Peter 2:9

But you are A CHOSEN RACE, A royal PRIESTHOOD, A HOLY
NATION, A PEOPLE FOR God's OWN POSSESSION, so that you may
proclaim the excellencies of Him who has called you out of darkness
into His marvelous light;

GOD APPOINTS

Acts 13:48

When the Gentiles heard this, they began rejoicing and glorifying the
word of the Lord; and as many as had been appointed to eternal life
believed.

1 Thessalonians 5:9

For God has not destined us for wrath, but for obtaining salvation
through our Lord Jesus Christ,

GOD PREDESTINES

Romans 8:29

For those whom He foreknew, He also predestined to become
conformed to the image of His Son, so that He would be the firstborn
among many brethren;

Ephesians 1:5 & 11

He predestined us to adoption as sons through Jesus Christ to
Himself, according to the kind intention of His will,.......also we have
obtained an inheritance, having been predestined according to His
purpose who works all things after the counsel of His will,

GOD PREPARES

Romans 9:23

> And He did so to make known the riches of His glory upon vessels of mercy, which He prepared beforehand for glory,

GOD CAUSES

1 Corinthians 1:30

> But by His doing you are in Christ Jesus, who became to us wisdom from God, and righteousness and sanctification, and redemption,

GOD CHOOSES

1 Thessalonians 1:4

> knowing, brethren beloved by God, His choice of you;

1 Thessalonians 2:13

> But we should always give thanks to God for you, brethren beloved by the Lord, because God has chosen you from the beginning for salvation through sanctification by the Spirit and faith in the truth.

Ephesians 1:4

> just as He chose us in Him before the foundation of the world, that we would be holy and blameless before Him In love

GOD PURPOSES

Ephesians 1:11

Paul, an apostle of Christ Jesus by the will of God, To the saints who are at Ephesus and who are faithful in Christ Jesus:

GOD DELIVERS AND TRANSFERS

Colossians 1:13

For He rescued us from the domain of darkness, and transferred us to the kingdom of His beloved Son,

GOD SAVES

2 Timothy 1:9

who has saved us and called us with a holy calling, not according to our works, but according to His own purpose and grace which was granted us in Christ Jesus from all eternity,

Titus 3:5

He saved us, not on the basis of deeds which we have done in righteousness, but according to His mercy, by the washing of regeneration and renewing by the Holy Spirit,

GOD MAKES US ALIVE

Ephesians 2:5

even when we were dead in our transgressions, made us alive together with Christ (by grace you have been saved),

GOD POURS OUT HIS SPIRIT

Titus 3:6

whom He poured out upon us richly through Jesus Christ our Savior,

GOD BRINGS US FORTH

James 1:18

In the exercise of His will He brought us forth by the word of truth, so that we would be a kind of first fruits among His creatures.

GOD JUSTIFIES

Romans 8:30

and these whom He predestined, He also called; and these whom He called, He also justified; and these whom He justified, He also glorified.

Titus 3:7

so that being justified by His grace we would be made heirs according to the hope of eternal life.

GOD SANCTIFIES

1 Thessalonians 5:23

Now may the God of peace Himself sanctify you entirely; and may your spirit and soul and body be preserved complete, without blame at the coming of our Lord Jesus Christ.

GOD GLORIFIES

Romans 8:3

> For what the Law could not do, weak as it was through the flesh, God did: sending His own Son in the likeness of sinful flesh and as an offering for sin, He condemned sin in the flesh,[ii]

As we can see, God is at work in all areas of salvation. He is the initiator as well as the accomplisher in every aspect. All glory is to be given to Him. We have absolutely zero room for boasting as we had nothing within us to save ourselves. Because of this work that God performs in us and around us, we can truly come to understand the plan of salvation.

That plan consists of calling, regeneration, faith, repentance, justification, adoption, sanctification, perseverance, and glorification.

In a nutshell:

First, we are called by God. He then regenerates us and gives us a nature of Christ. At this point, we are saved because we have been renewed. Upon this transformation, we immediately gain faith and cling to Him just as a newborn clings to his mother and father. It is at this point, and only at this point, that we now feel guilty of our past nature and confess it before God whereas before, we embraced the evil. Upon this point, we are justified of all wrongs because we now have an Advocate in Christ. We are then adopted into the family of God where we can cry Abba, Father. As new creatures in Christ we are fully sanctified and cleansed by the atoning blood of Christ. Those who belong to God and are given to the Son will persevere until the end for no one can snatch us out of the Father's hand and Jesus will not lose any that are given to him. Upon our entry into Heaven, we will then be glorified in our heavenly eternal state with God.

1 Corinthians 4:7

> For who regards you as superior? What do you have that you did not receive? And if you did receive it, why do you boast as if you had not received it?

2 Corinthians 10:17

> But HE WHO BOASTS IS TO BOAST IN THE LORD.

Steven Lawson

> The good news of the Bible is that God saves sinners. God the Father chose His elect, gave them to the Son, commissioned the Son to redeem them, and sends the Spirit to regenerate them. God the Son laid down His life for the sheep, securing their salvation. God the Spirit gives repentance, faith, and eternal life to these chosen ones. Salvation is a great work of the triune God's amazing grace. [iii]

Always remember, it is God who gets the credit. Outside of His will and plan, there is no salvation. To say we initiate our own salvation is to take glory away from God and apply it to ourselves. To say God is compelled to give us something if we ask for it makes God our servant and takes glory away from Him. To say God is only reactionary based on our choices removes His sovereignty. It is to say we are more powerful than God and that He must bend to our decrees and desires. This also robs God of His glory by giving it to ourselves. We have no reason to boast. Every single part of salvation was composed and orchestrated by God. Everything we have is only because we received it by a God who gave it to us.

Soli Deo Gloria! Glory to God alone!

[i] John MacArthur, The MacArthur Bible Commentary (1 Corinthians) [Thomas Nelson, 2005] pg. 1,567

[ii] ibid.

[iii] Steven Lawson, The Gospel Focus of Charles Spurgeon [Reformation Trust Publishing, 2012] pg. 58

INDEX OF SCRIPTURES

8:29	111
8:29-30	106
8:30	7, 67, 78, 114
9:15-16	108
9:16	55
9:18	108
9:23	108, 112
9:23-24	78
10:20	55
11:12	108

1 CORINTHIANS

1:30	104, 109, 112
2:10-13	75
2:14	45, 77, 105
3:10-15	27
3:15	20, 27
4:7	427 116
6:9-11	89
6:19	45
12:13	76

2 CORINTHIANS

3:5	47
5:8	25
5:17	76
10:17	116

GALATIANS

1:3-4	63
1:8-9	30
1:15-16	79
2:16	22
3:1-3	7
5:1	7

EPHESIANS

1:4	112

1:5	55, 109, 111
1:11	57, 109, 111, 113
1:13-14	86
1:17-18	77
2:1	43
2:3	105
2:5	113
2:8	4
2:10	57
4:4	79

PHILIPPIANS

1:6	87

COLOSSIANS

1:13	8, 113
1:13-14	66
1:21	105
2:10	8
2:13-14	8

1 THESSALONIANS

1:4	112
2:12	110
2:13	112
4:3	67
5:9	56, 111
5:23	90, 114

2 THESSALONIANS

2:3-4	99
2:10	99
2:14	110

HEBREWS

7:26-27	12
9:15	79
9:27	26
10:1	12
10:10-12	12

13:12	67

1 TIMOTHY

1:9	110
1:15	63
3:15	14
3:16	95
4:1	96, 97, 98
4:2	96
4:3	96, 97
4:6	100
4:16	102

2 TIMOTHY

1:9	55, 79, 113
3:16-17	100
4:18	91

TITUS

1:1	51
1:15	45
2:14	65
3:5	4, 113
3:6	114
3:7	114

1 PETER

1:1-2	51, 104
1:4-5	91
1:7	28
1:15	79, 81
1:20	53, 67, 107
2:8-9	56
2:9	79, 111

2 PETER

1:10	91
3:10	29

JAMES

1:18	114

ABOUT THE AUTHOR

Travis W. Rogers is a diligent student of the Word and has served in the U.S. Navy since 2000. From 2008-2012, he has acted as Protestant Lay Leader onboard the USS Benfold (DDG-65) and led others in their spiritual walk in the absence of a Chaplain. It has been his deepest desire to see others come to the knowledge of truth and experience a deeper walk with God. His previous works include "Wading In the Deep End: Difficulties In Scripture & Theology."

Travis and his wife, Tiffany, are blessed to have a son and two daughters.

Made in the USA
Charleston, SC
03 June 2013